# A VOYAGE OF MYSTERY

BEN

**BALBOA.**PRESS
A DIVISION OF HAY HOUSE

Balboa Press books may be ordered through booksellers or by contacting:

Balboa Press
A Division of Hay House
1663 Liberty Drive
Bloomington, IN 47403
www.balboapress.co.uk
UK TFN: 0800 0148647 (Toll Free inside the UK)
UK Local: (02) 0369 56325 (+44 20 3695 6325 from outside the UK)

Print information available on the last page.

ISBN: 978-1-9822-8461-9 (sc)
ISBN: 978-1-9822-8462-6 (e)

Balboa Press rev. date: 10/20/2021

# CONTENTS

Symbiosis ............................................................. xi

The title of this book is........................................... xiii

Author biography ................................................ xv

Introduction..................................................... xvii

Setting the scene ................................................... 1

The poem: Forfeit to the now ............................... 2

True originals......................................................... 4

Fledged ................................................................. 5

Life's delights ....................................................... 6

Planet of the sun .................................................. 7

Soul....................................................................... 8

Illusion.................................................................. 9

Fairy tales........................................................... 10

Not there............................................................ 11

Pleasures that are............................................... 12

Existence............................................................ 13

The ladder of life ............................................... 16

All for the job..................................................... 18

Streets of the lonesome ...................................... 19

Simple pleasures ................................................ 20

Personal walls..................................................... 21

The things that matter........................................ 22

Friendship .......................................................... 23

Dreams, or schemes............................................ 24

Morning glory.................................................... 25

Perfection of home ............................................................26
You............................................................................27
Symbiosis ...................................................................28
Flash mobs ..................................................................29
Real change..................................................................30
Justice .......................................................................31
Walkies ......................................................................32
Sunday roast.................................................................33
Leftovers .....................................................................35
Awaiting the light...........................................................36
Tandoori delight.............................................................37
Bottled hope.................................................................38
For some… the itch name ................................................39
Bean the cat .................................................................41
Life ...........................................................................42
Shame ........................................................................43
Enemy of old................................................................44
Life is ........................................................................45
True union ...................................................................46
Gone, but never forgotten ................................................48
Beaker of justice ............................................................49
Peace of mind................................................................50
Another day .................................................................51
Expectations.................................................................52
The last laugh ...............................................................53
Stolen moments.............................................................54
Stolen ........................................................................55
Random chances ............................................................56
Empowered ..................................................................57
Confidents always ..........................................................58
Mis-placed ...................................................................60
A small fortune .............................................................61
lies............................................................................62
Point of no-return ..........................................................63

Prime times ........................................................................64

Strategy ..............................................................................65

Walking on air ...................................................................66

Empty plate ........................................................................67

Jigsaw puzzle .....................................................................68

My bird ...............................................................................69

Friends ................................................................................70

Consideration .....................................................................71

Dis-functional ....................................................................72

Chess ...................................................................................73

The watched clock .............................................................74

My true love .......................................................................76

Last orders ..........................................................................77

That competition ...............................................................78

True essence ........................................................................80

The Beast of tipsy moor ....................................................81

Arguments ..........................................................................83

Pillows .................................................................................84

The tipping point ..............................................................85

Fresh water .........................................................................86

Beginnings ..........................................................................87

The sun to cheer ................................................................89

Forgotten promises ............................................................90

Promises and lies ...............................................................91

My rusty nail ......................................................................93

Cry of nature ......................................................................94

Choices ................................................................................95

Equality ...............................................................................96

Tentative steps ...................................................................97

Leverage ..............................................................................99

Phased in mind ................................................................100

Trifling matters ................................................................101

Insurance ..........................................................................102

Moral fibre ........................................................................103

Hitting the high notes .................................................. 104
Brewing time ................................................................ 105
Value ............................................................................ 106
Insidious ...................................................................... 107
Elevation ...................................................................... 108
Ominous ...................................................................... 109
That 'feeling of knowing' ............................................ 110
Curtains drawn ............................................................ 111
Winds of change .......................................................... 112
Small fry ...................................................................... 113
Ice ................................................................................ 115
Quick snacks ................................................................ 117
Life's blood .................................................................. 118
Balancing the equation ................................................ 120
True power .................................................................... 122
Commitment ................................................................ 123
The friendship of science ............................................ 124
Irony of life .................................................................. 125
The falls ........................................................................ 126
Thirst ............................................................................ 127
Rectify that which is wrong ........................................ 128
Why be sad .................................................................. 129
Shifting ideas .............................................................. 130
Our future truth .......................................................... 131
Personal data .............................................................. 132
Wafer thin .................................................................... 133
The radical that be ...................................................... 134
Caution the play .......................................................... 135
Attention to the detail ................................................ 136
Roots ............................................................................ 137
Ethics ............................................................................ 139
Swings and roundabouts ............................................ 140
The lawn of delight ...................................................... 141
Character built ............................................................ 142

Trust of the system..................................................143
Mystery of the woods............................................144
True fear ..................................................................146
Time of us...............................................................148
Profitability ...........................................................150
Respect of life........................................................152
Toast.......................................................................153
Coping mechanisms...............................................154
Autumn now...........................................................155
Candour..................................................................156
The long game........................................................157
Family.....................................................................158
Above and beyond..................................................159
Beating hearts fire .................................................160

Acknowledgements.................................................163
Authors final message............................................165

# SYMBIOSIS

This book has 138 poems. All the work offered are original, written by my hand. In total there are 183 pages of text! The design of the book is of differing styles. However, though the greatest bulk of this offering is new work within a period of four months. Earlier poems included, add to the essence that I wished to convey.

# THE TITLE OF THIS BOOK IS.

A voyage of mystery

This book is about emotions. I have written upon a vast numbers of genres, so many close to my heart! My offerings are in a four-stanza form. However, in order to show diversity, other methods of presentation occur. Ranging through a full course of emotion, I hope you enjoy. Hoped is that this book will take you to places you may never have ever been!

# AUTHOR BIOGRAPHY

I am quiet by nature, but a drink does raise my voice. Writing has not been a large part of my life, but I am able to produce words arranged in new forms. The pen now enriches my days, Even using dream mechanisms to write from my sleep.

The youngest of six children, my family has always been there for me. This despite my farther leaving my mother when still incredibly young. During working times, jobs include manual work. Never a person with full capabilities, my output limited! The greener grass wanted, but so seldom found.

Now older I write again… this after a break for fifteen years. I write as one of you. All that can be I am for those that do become emersed. Emotions are a humans greatest show of feeling! Hoped is the fact that this voyage of words will Take you to a special place.

# INTRODUCTION

Come ride upon the surf with me:
Highs, and lows you shall feel, and see!
Board below, this othering is for you:
Brave waves create this as you read true!

Told are stories through poetic verse:
Giggles erupt, I hope you need no nurse!
Smiles: hope is… this voyage give to you:
Known is poems shall ring true!

This offering is for everyone; I hope you enjoy

Now the poetry begins

# SETTING THE SCENE

Light does capture, silhouetted are things hardly seen:
The illumination here is the theme!
Candle's flicker, these create diffused scene:
Imagination churning, thoughts dull, then gleam!

Creation of writing new, this the reason for lighting of room:
New combinations of words, from pen boom!
Rhyme the biggest factor of... what shall I pen:
Time eventually brings new fruit to end!

Dancing shadows stimulate, the scent here too:
Speed of hand form now, lines which I do view!
This like other combinations, is destined for the dark:
Confidence of ability trust, within others one day park!

Merits of the finished, one day scrutinized:
I hope bring pleasure, certainly make surprised!
Whatever the outcome... pattern of; did please my eye:
Happy with; my creation shall remain... upon paper surprise!

# THE POEM: FORFEIT TO THE NOW

Forfeit to the now, mind is as fire:
Writing poetry, this is my only desire!
Intense thoughts begin to flavour me write:
few words wrong, others so right!

Dancing thoughts echoed by the performance upon walls:
Majesty of imagination, this with pen falls
Chaotic is the ambience, flickering the candle flames:
Here, now begins the poetry games!

Tingling vibrations ignite word brew:
Sentences light hoped not to transform to stew!
Only capture essence of what is the now:
Simplicity of words, 'key' measure to wow!

Hands form shadows, this as they parade within candlelight:
Dark areas make right this night!
Patterns continuously changing, are a delight:
The now is joyous, here there is no plight!

Forming sentences begin to true ring:
I here as if music, as if someone does sing!
Only when a smile does ping:
That moment of aspiration, chime through life's ding!

Emotions now are in true flow:
But still, there is a long way to go!
With head, and body done, only legs to complete:
Last verse raise poem to feet!

Vibrant, flamboyant, such words are in brain:
This poem for me is both, I do not want to tame!
Onward with conviction, this poem must become complete:
Must stand, even run upon feet!

Poignancy, this as poem enters last verse:
Candles shuddering, the light has never been worse!
As upon all, the flames do die:
Last line penned, I feel that I could fly!

# TRUE ORIGINALS

Fluid in thought, this as fledglings flew from nest:
Ideas rushing, image of new, held to chest!
Paper, or canvas where originality fly:
Non-biological art forms never die!

Success of longevity, viewing of human eye:
Uniqueness bring tear, even real cry!
If true to person... for a second, may ride upon wave crest:
Soul; even for a moment, lain to rest!

Search for inspiration, goal of any artiste quest:
Formulation writing or illustration, viewers mind knows best!
Birds now the greatest determiners... reason for why:
Generations of the people could but try!

Art must travel, from one society to the next:
Viewed through flavours, thought upon held... chest!
If any appreciator's, birds continually fly:
If not, or lost, artwork memory of... die!

# FLEDGED

A new direction, in life to follow:
Not today but starting tomorrow!
Within dreamscape inspiration aroused:
Tantalising ideas that could empowered allow!

Not could, should, become exposed, stay:
It is me that must initialize their play!
Likened to bird nest, fledglings need to fly:
Activation of… one can but try!

Months have flown, this since first tentative step:
Forming is the outcome, but more time needed yet!
Dough rounded, baking still to go:
Now in oven, raising seems so slow!

Now fledged, this book is the cooked cake:
You are the voice of any impact it does make!
Feelings of joy to the multitude bring:
My words chorused, hoped not had their final sing!

# LIFE'S DELIGHTS

Teased by the aroma, my nose does twitch:
Upon viewing, my choice of purchase enriched!
My eyes tell the story of personal glee:
But which, which will embrace with me!

Price yes, this is a major concern:
Check of pockets, three pound sixty to churn!
Off my menu so much a thing:
But now spotted that one tantalising ring!

A pastry, which looks like a work of art:
Tongue caresses lips as footsteps start!
Now within shop, money in hand:
Pointed out that which looks so grand!

One last smell, this before first bite:
Yes, this choice is so right!
Now devoured, crumbs removed by hand:
Even though seated, my body does stand!

# PLANET OF THE SUN

The restoration of our planet, this will not occur overnight:
It may take generations, to put human arrogance right!
Our very being, has been to raid Earth resources for worth:
Now enlightened; those realise this was for the worse!

We have taken so much; shall take even more:
Such are demands of humanity, ignorance of taking never cure!
Removal of the harmful, this needs quickly done:
Use truly practical alternatives, save our
biological 'planet of the sun'!

We have raped mother, but still; she is not barren dry:
New policies of support, allow reversal of today's cry!
Essence of mother nature, we need to with the supporting, comply:
Not just to create a better world, but to fortify!

As a species, we might have potential:
If humanity is to thrive... Earths care is essential!
Facts of harming, these do not need verified:
We have the knowledge, now wisdom must be to be complied!

# SOUL

My soul I believe has existed, since long ago:
Memories not mine invigorate, also cause low!
Know do I, that I am not alone:
But in past was a commoner, never sat upon any throne!

Of... life's before, have no real memory:
My body is this, I make no enemy!
Quiet is my nature, adventurous my soul:
Shade is my comfort, never have I eaten from cherry bowl!

To brieve the air, simply to be:
In truth it is not enough, but this is me!
Want... yes, I have passions... needs:
My measure will be result of deeds!

Hurt... I think to others, this impossible for me:
Sometimes life gets in the way, my response... please!
Each are different... have pleasure, but also will mourn:
When this frame gone, trust another born!

# ILLUSION

...It is the mystery; we see what is not true:
But illusion, this be the greatest pounder, of or you!
The way that we are deceived:
Great upon stage, how even perceived!

An illusion, have in current day seam surreal:
...If life was, change the course of the real!
Attenders of shows, they are the truest believers of all:
The partitioners of; their heads stand tall!

Mirrors, these used during the greatest illusions of all:
What we do not see, this is a practitioners best tool!
We are but puppets in their game:
We the mesmerised... enjoy their aim!

Past, is past, but there is a new theme:
Upon stage, they are the singers of a dream!
Entertainment is simply part of a myriad nature:
We are all mother's, susceptible to any creator!

# FAIRY TALES

Fingers crossed, my aspirations, wants, needs, now real:
Nonsense, but from that world, for moment dream steal!
Peace for a while, dreams can be that:
All play in the imaginary, live in the world of non-fact!

Would be nice if each could live their dream:
Take an absence from life's real theme!
...But fairy tales are not real, just fables told:
So many loved, by young, and old!

Feeling: this is the measure, of what one can perceive:
But sometimes, words designed to deceive!
We read, laugh, also scowl:
Humanity can be good, but at times fowl!

The greatest writer, introduce gruesome, or love, they do:
Those of past, only knowers of what might be true!
Words written... these record so much of the human song:
Through their authors, the show must go on!

# NOT THERE

Trance like, this now is a world of their own:
Head still, eyes glazed, nothing seems to be known!
What the reason, obviously drug partaken:
All I can say, upon my watch any such soul never forsaken!

Now rocking, only thing to do ... watch:
Tears falling, this upon down-slope another notch!
Help... there is little, if any:
These times now in truth to them an enemy!

Morning now, through exhaustion got winks:
Not really washed, but not sure who stinks!
Food, this these days is an alien thing:
Wish is... for intervention to begin!

But no; it seems this is my burden... I am on my own:
Just so many others, put through same life poem!
I just hope, my conviction to the escape cause... truly bloom:
Come back to the functioning Earth, my loved ones soon!

# PLEASURES THAT ARE

Tantalising now, ridiculous, these aromas have persuaded tongue:
Hunger the obvious, soon eating done!
But another alcoholic drink first' this is such a time:
Soon combination of, the perfect rhyme!

Content now, my stomach is fill:
Another drink, do I need this still?
Tonight, the answer not, I need to get home:
Bed awaits, aspiration now of... that memory foam!

Now mattress has returned, before my body lay:
Coffee needed, just to start the day!
Mind crowded by the awakening fog:
Let out must be my beloved dog!

Necessary done, again within home 'heart' soon to return':
Pats, rubs, water partaken of, soon walkies earn!
Such is life, all have their own ways:
...Ours is to enjoy, if possible, absorb such days!

# EXISTENCE

Known is… one day this frame will simply fail:
My existence be at an end!
But my soul, except this will go into future new:
Abundance of the biological added too!

Hope is this soul has gained from me:
Enriched by what I done or did see!
Give sturdy platform for the next that be:
Achieve beyond that which was me!

Upon greeting those of family that passed before:
Knowledge of earlier ended for evermore!
My uniqueness, this be in spirit form:
Lighter, but heart by knowledge not warmed!

Needs of the living, these just matter now:
No sustenance needed but will miss the Capow!
Of Earth, hoped is the nursery survive, and thrive:
Dead at present but might again become alive!

# RHYTHM IN FLOW

Embroiled in the moment, but now that inspiration is gone:
Embers stay, these fanned... formed into poem!
Fire shall be the feature, this element become inflamed:
At conclusion, it's veracity tamed!

Smoke now, this as heat does fade:
But now from ashes a new fire made!
Kindling added, this to encourage first sparks:
More combustible material added, flames as fire starts!

Warmth now, this elevates the room:
Signs of relief as clothes heavy, come off soon!
Now raging, all logs now alight:
Increasing smiles radiate, this temperature is right!

Conversation elevated, the banter goes on, and on:
But now all the burnable is gone!
Still though the blazing fire, it's voracity continues from:
Dancing shadows, they silhouette, play as if song!

later now, chatter has reducer echoing that of flames:
Temperature is dropping, the assembled have new aims!
Thick clothing again worn; the fire fury tamed:
Enthusiasm for this night now waned!

Nature is nature, this governs us all:
Time is the factor, Mothers greatest call!
Flowed have words, flourished into life:
The pen is mighty, but not compared to wife!

# The ladder of life

Result of union, new to soon to begin:
Baby kicking, soon from womb spring!
Birthed now, hundreds of tears fall:
Mother elixir aids the growth wall!

Solids, and fluids given, now raised to legs:
Soon so hard to catch, to peg!
Much faster now, sneaky too:
Adolescence is the new brew!

What are my limits, what can I do?
Test is the measure, always try the new!
Teenage so quick, the years have flown:
Tricks so plentiful, within life have been inter-woven!

Mantle now changes, time is now to earn respect:
Time now will decide what I might get!
Accomplished or not, yours is where you are:
Luck, or money, your car is your car!
Health now not as good as before:
Failing of youths brightness, smiles little more!
Grimm reaper knocks upon the door:
Was life good, did I choose correct, really explore?

We each have our passage, moment in time:
Born to die, sometimes do chime!
Make that mark, which says this was me:
If known, pass on legacy to those that still be!

# ALL FOR THE JOB

Running now for station... rain caught me unaware:
Got there eventually, for work though I do not care!
Soaked by my own misunderstanding:
Thought rain not due... but gave me a real pounding!

Now bedraggled upon crowded train I stand:
...Of this journey I am not grand!
But must is must, workplace must make:
Living is upon biscuits; I want to eat cake!

This travel does have its calm:
Gave a possible seat to the first woman!
Shivery always my nature... parents taught me that:
Honest living... brought up with that fact!

Arrival for work now, on time for a change:
Multitude of faces welcome, but now much to arrange!
In truth... drudgery really, but this is my life:
At least when home... get kisses from wife!

# STREETS OF THE LONESOME

I wonder the 'streets of the lonesome':
Have visited places, few will ever see!
Area dark by their very nature:
But in truth multitudes exist, deprived of stature!

Even within the fairest of societies:
There are always those left behind!
Any street might have similar houses:
But occupiers, economically vastly different will find!

Council, or private, factor does show personal wealth:
Just having roof, this fact the majority toast!
With financial liquidity one can keep personal health:
Without illness promoted, there are no benefits of coast!

Summer is close, but the sea so far away.
Want might be its tranquillity, but no ability to for pay!
…And so, upon the 'streets of the lonesome', the multitude stay:
Perhaps in time, have their way!

# SIMPLE PLEASURES

It is the smallest of ideas that can endear the most:
Simplicity of even receiving piece of toast!
Gesture from others that show you respect:
In life we know, you get what you get!

Pleasures are myriad, they vary one to another:
What is good for one, not for the other!
Completing that job that no one else can do:
Even first sip of that cocktail new!

Life gives, and takes, each and every day:
Millions work, others at home they stay!
Into the unknown we must venture:
But moments occur, they are random by nature!

Perhaps taking part in a sport, that other would raise their brow:
Tap glasses to an occasion, to cheer even howl!
Our world filled with mystery; simple pleasures top our day:
Without life is hollow, there would be no pay!

# PERSONAL WALLS

We all have that place which is our own:
Within even those most loved, not allowed to roam!
It is a person's barrier, which supports sanity:
Keeps us part of true humanity!

Ours is ours, each need their own space:
But sorting problems out, should not be in haste!
Alone we might feel, but another can help solve:
Life from that which is… revolve!

White lies are told, these to help those we hold close:
Perhaps, cheeky methods to console, those we love most!
…But their personal walls… upon we might encroach:
By intervention, viewed only as cockroach!

Personal walls help us to life hold:
Continuity, this too life quality be bold!
Breaching another's walls; this is a human trait:
Numerous numbers of people, for their life to create!

# THE THINGS THAT MATTER

Grow out with wrongs foods, up when right:
Genes the determiner of day and night!
We cannot change who we are meant to be:
But millions do enhance cosmetically!

Diets yes, these used to ease the bulge:
Even a pound to millions, changer of mould!
Truth is that weight might hinder functionality:
But it is not the figure that matters, it is the personality!

Being honest to oneself, this is the way to be:
Those who say yes, say this to me!
Find those where acceptance is realities of life:
Do not judge, just love concept like husband, or wife!

None are always perfect in body, or attitude:
Blemishes of skin, marks upon figure, or amplitude!
Forest that is life traversed by all:
No matter if thin, fat, or marked, in life stand tall!

# FRIENDSHIP

Whispers unheard, but known are about you:
Sometimes true!
That uneasy feeling, are you wrong?
But now in head song!

Words spoken towards you direction start the rot:
Cause harm which adds to life's pot!
Even with best friends arguments occur:
Needed so much, but like cat do purr!

millions talk, rubbishing others is their way:
Thousands in quiet listen to the day!
Smell the truth, believe only in real fact:
Friends may change, but life is about that!

That person always ready for a chat:
Humanity at the best, this is that!
Smiles can replace any heart that does burn:
Happiness replace the sad, this often will return!

# DREAMS, OR SCHEMES

Dreams are dreams, but schemes are schemes:
Those that are dishonest, they are of life a constant theme!
All dream, millions scheme, but it is for life to be supreme:
But we all know, for society the high is a dream!

The schemers, they have a manipulative way:
Moral compass point direction of deceiving play!
Ability to hoax, makes their pay:
For a while, the majority enjoy the light of day!

Dreamers are us all, there is always that thing out of reach:
For the higher educated, they have the ability to teach!
Child to parent, tell of shackles they cannot breach:
Tell of times where glass ceiling they could not impeach!

Whatever your nature, of humanity we are all part:
Living is the challenge, from life's very start!
Thousands have changes, others not even if smart:
Time is the process where you get to fill your shopping cart!

# MORNING GLORY

Upon awakening the first cupper is new dream:
Without cannot function, amber nectar needed for day to begin!
Sat supping, haze of night begins to lift:
Soon my body able to shift!

Day ahead, now can at least bare:
… Of chore drudgery, in truth do not care!
Finished now, all housework is done:
This day at conclusion, hope that I won!

Washed, dressed, invigored too go:
Dog: walk now, whom I talk, never know!
Single, this might be that day?
Not on websites, believe life… meeting the true stay!

Hope is the essence of my life:
What will be, who knows, could be my soul mate… wife?
Simple hello's, perhaps wave:
Little chats that make the day!

# PERFECTION OF HOME

Passion is burning, but this is not for the sexual kind of love:
It is that item that endears, this to elevate as Dove!
That little piece that is missing from home:
For which would reveal deepest secret, this for dome!

Life is we need; small things create the perfect home:
That one ornament that stands alone!
Maybe a picture that compliments a wall:
...Or outdoor adornment that makes you walk tall!

Proud is the greatest feeling, all should feel at least that:
We crave joy during life, this is a fact!
Maybe getting that bargain, before anyone else did grab:
...Upon receiving, that which you never had!

Such is such, we all have our dreams:
The majority adorn with the community themes!
Dream we do, but only the few have their perfect house:
...within there can never be like mine a mouse!

Care of domain, people as a concept do:
This the place where a cooked meal for, invited few!
Clean is best as that says that of property you really care:
When work seems overpowering never despair!

# YOU

You think yourself as nothing... not true!
You are the best of me... and you!
Like peas in pod, we were meant to be together:
Enjoy showers, which are not part of weather!

Storms of life are commonplace:
We could not survive if there was no chase!
Simply brave the struggles that are now, and ahead:
Together we shall make our bread!

Upon awakening, that first kiss is worth the wait:
Smile do I, appreciate!
Know that in life, currently I have won:
Overflowing, in love my brain... over run!

You whisper, my skin hairs raise:
For the warmth of your body, in a daze!
Without am nothing, from life vade:
With... bed of contentment always made!

# SYMBIOSIS

Upon life's journey, there are billions of paths to take:
It is our symbiosis with others, this that simplification make!
Only route forward travelled by everyone:
Destination who knows where, that is your song!

Stumbles there will be, scrapes, and bruises part:
All decisions become items in personal cart!
This cart is never filled, there is always room for more:
hundreds get heavy, for the majority it's wheels light to floor!

Within nature, true symbiosis is simply the needed thing:
Even if not beneficial to both, it is how Mother does sing!
Bees as they visit pollen givers, example of themes:
Plover bird in crocodile mouth, strange are Earth scenes!

…Of humanity, devotion as two become one:
Even life given, to protect highest of throne!
In truth, myriad are symbiotic relationships, presence vast:
Bit-parts of life… must be if it is to last!

# FLASH MOBS

Flash mobs, what brilliance do they scheme?
Inspiration is their dream!
Those that together surprise at what they bring:
United, music to all heart's play, and sing!

Military or not, they are the newest quest:
Peace to all, they play from chest!
Maybe impossible in this current day:
In future must be, this if true humanity is to stay!

Music expresses what we are:
It might be to ear rubbish, even if best of choir!
Each perceive music in their own way:
Life is this… is the human say!

Together we clan, to common cause:
Others might perceive but hear as noise!
Thousands of singers have good voice:
Whatever the sound it is your choice!

# REAL CHANGE

From acorns grows the mighty Oak tree:
From spawn frogs come to be!
Cycles of life are Earths common theme:
But we as humans have the ability to dream!

We surpass other species due to brain:
Even our collective knowledge, the environment can never tame!
But we are learning, humanity is still young:
As a species we are at risk, fact until real progress done!

Green the new buzzword, this after so often Brown:
Greening of our planet, worn still a very loose crown!
Targets for improvement set, but will any be reached?
Or will cost result in promises being beached?

Whales even get lost, this despite vastness of oceans, and seas:
Earth is fragile, humanities activity cannot be as our species please!
New generations should not have to fix activity of the before:
But have to, this if humanity continue for evermore!

# JUSTICE

Euphoric was the occasion, but sad the times:
Governmental policies, only rhythms, and rhymes!
For now, the issue was addressed:
But before, there was multitude of arrest!

Rebellion… not against law, but what is wrong:
People millions singing a continuous song!
"We want justice, we want truth":
Call of those, who need to see the proof!

Court's judge, but do they hear the real fact:
Money buys freedom, we all know that!
Pay pence for trial, you get a child:
If you have the money… thrive in the while!

Maybe laugh, get away with what was done:
In past, billions corrupt have won!
With power, there should be true responsibility:
Changes are ahead, but we will see!

# WALKIES

Say the word, which is all you need to do:
Bark of delight, wagging tail, attention only for you!
"Where is it, get your lead", these words spoken:
Sleepy heads often, but now dog is truly awoken!

Harness's and leads on, it is time to go:
Anticipation of outdoors, body trembling, they know!
Upon route now, of course with bag, or scoop in hand:
Your baby has learned where to stop and stand!

If male, any lamppost will receive attention:
Grassed areas the choice for crouching intention!
Marking territories, the constant theme, other need to know:
This place is mine, saying their show!

Now home, any collections placed in relevant bin:
Smiles abundant, even dog seems to grin!
Feeding now, water is already done:
Doggie again asleep, walkies were the doggie's crown!

# SUNDAY ROAST

Preparation first, but the result is worth the wait:
Aromas from kitchen supremely great!
Spuds from oven, inside soft outside crisp:
Sprouts boiled soft, salted to taste left Wisp!
Peas, and sweetcorn also boiled exactly right:
Strained and buttered what a sight!

Carrots, parsnips, also roasted but with 'honey and mustard' glaze:
Strangers walking past, tantalising air do amaze!
Gravy reduced, made from meat juice:
Upon dishing family let loose!
Condiments ready to add to filled plate:
Just by seeing, you know you can no longer wait!

Forgotten the Yorkshire puddings, these a must:
Batter quickly made, poured, cooked at
two twenty raising must trust!
Now readied… from oven strait to plates:
Smiles in abandon, these one of traditions greats!
After the devouring follows the sleepy times:
Afters maybe, but stomach happiness chimes!
Upon awaking picking of any morsels left:

Roasties always, these are the best!
Now the sweet pudding has room to tummy fit:
Giggles of excitement this also a hit!
Wow expressed to chef, all eyes gleam:
Family after roast the closest team!

# LEFTOVERS

What to do when eating is complete?
So much washing up, now to defeat!
But also, all that left over food:
It can be complexing, what to do?

For now, the fridge is the answer to the riddle game:
Out of sight, a nod... that is the aim!
Later now, all the related cooking chores done:
Family members again appear... each, and everyone!

You thought kitchen was closed for the night:
But now it is the leftovers, that again will delight!
Eggs have sat in their tray for too long:
Now shall be beaten, added the leftovers... this never wrong!

Puffed beauties, few... begin to appear from the frying pan:
Thoughts sometimes, 'how industrious I am'!
Again, with glee, all the edible does disappear:
This time washing up, not so severe!

# AWAITING THE LIGHT

As tides swept to shore, the sands seemed to be eroded:
Shafts of light appeared through fog; sunshine exploded!
Sand claimed for now by vastness of sea:
Calm of tranquillity here, I wish all could breathe!

Others appear, each partake of the morning air:
The morning larkers that, for the environment really care!
Soundtrack that of Gulls, shrieking as they plunder their finds:
This as the waves seem to rewind!

Warming rays begin radiating to face:
Coat removed, but there is no haste!
Basking soon as golden sands begin to gimmer:
...Of humans numbers are amassing, time away from dither!

Moment of first light, this now cherished throughout day:
Soul contented... for Mother's beauty there's no need to pay!
Fleeting images invigorate, beach but one scene:
Nature's raw magnificence is real, not just a dream!

# TANDOORI DELIGHT

Ingredients of Tandoori; very presence, fragrances the air:
Indian spices marinating the chicken, I can but glare!
Tantalisation, this even before being cooked:
My ticket for a tasting is truly booked!

...In oven now, aromas here exponentially multiply:
Tongue can taste, this ... as comes the tears from cry!
Mouth expectant of that Tandoori delight:
Hardships of day shall soon be put right!

Paid for; that exotic beauty is now within hands:
Behind me, thousand more lip moistening fans!
In envy, watched as I take my first bite:
It is time to disappear into the night!

Upon returning home, known today... my stomach has won:
Treated to perfection, that only monthly is done!
Funds are low, but all should indulge with favourite meal:
From doldrums, this is when time is real!

# BOTTLED HOPE

...If only hope could be bottled, opened when time's sad:
Like fine wine... mature, over time never go bad!
All keep at least one bottle of... this for that looming day:
Unlike 'Pandoras box', refresh the air upon
opening... smile again play!

So many factors decide life that be:
Hardships in life will always affect the majority!
Financial juggling must be the greatest concern of all:
Into depression so many do fall!

Time decide; how deep, how low, emotions become entrenched:
Life during, your essence benched!
...If only that bottle could see the light:
It's very presence might, fight from freedom from ignite!

Hope so often is the greatest emotional gain:
Only if there, then reduced is any pain!
Bottled I know, this is just a whimsical dream:
...But opening lid of, this could begin that theme!

# FOR SOME... THE ITCH NAME

Resistance was strong... this to Mary's call to the wild:
Life had been cosy, temptation never too inner child!
The urge to roam was now the quest:
Safety worry concerns of family, could not rest!

The world awaited an adventure so new:
Bug had bitten, alone travel Mary would do!
Communication fluid, at least the facts were made:
... And so, truce though sketchy, journey was for paid!

Asia the question, what truth's aspirational did hide?
What calm of spirit could this continent provide?
Order, pace of countries, there was a rigid plan:
But room for variation, part promise made to clan!

One month passed, all had gone well:
By now Mary was under Asia's spell!
Mesmerised... her appreciation of orient only smiles:
Vacation of Mary's life had taken her miles!

Upon route, family had been following path:
Between Mary and family, thousand a laugh!
Photographs sent, there had been hundred a chat:
Few lows, simple tranquillity... simply that!

Journey at end, airport now arrived:
Itch scratched; Mary had thrived!
Home now, family hugs of plenty:
Mary's fuel tank for exploration now empty!

# BEAN THE CAT

Startled, 'Bean' the cat for an instant froze:
Now came twitching of his nose!
Heart palpitating head turning rapidly left to right:
Now the time 'flight or fight'!

Flight the choice in a moment Bean had flown:
Fleet of foot but bravery was still not grown!
Still young Bean was still to set up his territory:
Within the cat domain there was an enemy!

Two years passed Bean had sprouted:
Matured now his vocals as if had shouted!
Came point of 'flight or fight' again:
Territory proved this now his sole domain!

Fight the answer, strength had to be shown:
The best of commitment had to be thrown!
A hundred scratches cut one or two:
Bean did proudly roam after he had won through!

# LIFE

Screams of inner emotion, heard by none:
Brewing's of life's harshness, come to point of done!
In secret, outing of pent-up stress is no fun:
After though, small victories of self-won!

All go through anguish, all pain:
Life should not be about losing, rather gain!
But life is simply, is what it is:
We are born, millions take, billions give!

Even the best known, these can rise from nothing:
Privileged by birth, always have something!
Those that do, these become the known:
Within societies fabric become inter-woven!

Only thousands might realise any unique moment of fame:
Once in limelight, hundreds be quickly tamed!
Speciality of talent can be a onetime wonder:
Throughout life there is much to ponder!

# SHAME

Poor of the poor… those are the multitude, worldwide shame:
Poorness increasing, this as rich gain!
…If only levelled, is the under paid game:
Against those, hold head in shame!

Family; so often… so far away!
Members here, deserve to stay:
What is needed is… those that want to work:
Be employed, hopefully, respectability book!

Only the few, our own, our real evil!
Those that deny, think current times not real!
Doubt is everywhere, in democracy… is the right:
If together all can put wrong to the night!

All we are… is who will be:
This time is ours, will be in history!
Equality is the only answer, but long time away:
But in future that will be the day!

# ENEMY OF OLD

We might meet, but ideals of never greet:
All we can do is... stand upon own feet!
Their attitude, simply different from your own:
That little thing, which do not like... is known!

True friends are those, that see life as the same:
Against there is no need to aim!
Co-existence, living life with a common laugh:
What can be better, than sometimes being loved as daft!

Uniqueness is ours, we all certainly have that:
As adult, we are not child... needed is real chat!
In truth, there is always that with... cannot get along:
Family even... this is life's song!

Everyone has uniqueness, even in the closest of society:
Each are each... this is whom we be!
Enemies are enemies, sometimes ponderance is why?
For betterment... wish all could try!

# LIFE IS

My babies are K-nines, of human babies I have none:
Not sure why but reminiscence is of times of fun!
Tobacco no, but from alcohol I do not shun:
Upon looking backwards through time, think that I have run!

I have swum in sea mile off sandy edge:
To others viewed as harmful, never given my pledge!
Money no, never have I needed a wedge:
Smiles even when through lows I did dredge!

My pledge can be given to any good cause:
If not money, then certainly applause!
Those that pursuit is for desperation to change:
Honours should have a long range!

Bad times have been, still they be:
Such are past, but in future again see!
Life is… complex, million stones hinder the road:
Calamitous if you need to be towed!

But your life is for you to decide:
Play it straight, or from illegally let provide!
Always hold your cards tight to chest:
…Or play it bold, try to get hold of the rest!

# True union

Only ten socially apart but spirit of same million:
Voices raised, heard as if billion!
Bonded this day, to injustice all arose:
Against combat, all opposed!

Glasses, trophies held so high:
Here we stood for others to survive!
Visual this… no place to hide:
This true show of pride!

Hooters sounded for our collective union:
Echoed for collected minion!

We did not walk, rather together formed:
Had no weapons but were forewarned!
Police here nodded this as truth dawned:
No emotions had been pawned!

Hooters sounded for our collective union:
Echoed for collected minion!

Hope the only armer worn:
Cloak of union now born!
Unity of the now never be torn:
Wrongs righted... never mourned!

So many protestors told, "go home":
"Negative resources" for any zone!
Contact direct, often cannot by phone:
In protest must roam!

# GONE, BUT NEVER FORGOTTEN

In an instance, a life was gone:
Not yours, or mine… but that of a loved one!
Now in dream, even when awake:
Laughter, and tears… remembrance create!

Regret do I, hundreds a mistake:
Plans that we made, risks did take!
…With fondness, face now a flood:
Know this, your life was no dud!

You enriched, certainly me:
Gave of yourself… cast net wide, fact that be!
But now, you are not there:
Home when passing, always stare!

Cherished by friends… family too:
Highlight of any party, this was you!
Gathered now, this for wake of goodbye:
Faces tell story, honour of your why!

# BEAKER OF JUSTICE

The beaker of justice… this from so often sipped:
Even a spelling mistake, justice has slipped!
So many a crime, but how do avoider of justice get to be punished?
Details of… these so often only rubbished!

Caught in the act, this much harder to defend:
Laugh at the evidence, this the trend!
Witnesses state, "at 'time of crime; charged was with them":
…If believed, so hard for charges to to upend!

So, few judges, too many a crime:
…In life this is the world's true rhyme!
But real is the fact that prisons are full:
We must trust in our system of fair trial for all!

The beaker is the giver of justice, sipping occurs much:
But no gulps taken, such hope just courage…Dutch!
Beaker never near empty, justice at certain points needs a crutch:
We are, where we are, such is such!

# PEACE OF MIND

Tranquillity even for a moment, can bring peace of mind:
A break from normality... smile to find!
Pleasure of being present, at exactly the correct time:
Instant where everything is simply sublime:

Seconds of intake, of the mown grass scented air:
Solution to puzzle, which for so long you could but stare!
Feeling when known all chores are done:
Even the watching of setting, or rising, sun!

Winning that final, becoming the exalted one:
Telling that story, where all stay... no one gone!
Getting that special thing, that your mouth does for pine:
...Or writing, lines that rhyme!

Pleasure is myriad, contentment often seen:
All are bit-parts, in what can seem like dream!
Life is for living; we get but one trial:
Peace of mind should be for all, at least for a while!

# ANOTHER DAY

Another day, in this life of bore:
As in sleep, I wish to snore!
Life before, was not just sleep:
But by government, are we sheep?

Times are a changing, new freedoms won:
Our efforts... these not yet though done!
No longer are confines of home:
But still, there is no true freedom to roam!

Most still will not make that to outside step:
I agree, this Covid is not over yet!
I disagree with those that say "no threat":
Hope is... they come to no regret!

This poem is... riddle of our time:
Each going through, changing of its rhyme!
Known only, at climax humanity again win:
But for loss, what song shall we sing?

# EXPECTATIONS

Gate old, but foreboding, stood strong as if new:
Barrier not to be crossed… no entry through!
…For so long; upon hinges had remained strong:
Cemented in position, time here simply marches on!

Beyond gate, large house left in disrepair:
Only via back does anything, or one, make it there!
Bastille now, this home is to isolate:
Owner will not leave, has learnt to hermit ate!

Likened to 'great expectations'… real truth of many a home:
Jilted by most significant other, no place from to roam!
'Lamb in life', abandonment is the most bitter of all torment:
Heart-broken. Usually life's last lament!

Now grinding, this as key turns… gate opens slow:
Occupant has died, body to morgue must go!
Always from lie's ashes, a Félix may arise:
Misery can be replaced by many a surprise!

# THE LAST LAUGH

Laughter... this can be the most contagious of things:
Even occurs as awakened from dreams!
Marker of joy, I am sure... is not a human only ability?
Does a dog smile before eyes... we simply do not see?

They that laugh loudest, they may bring cheer:
Reason for volume, this is never clear!
Loudest are they who have imposing personality:
Others quietly laugh, that is the way they be!

To each their own, all should in laugh indulge:
Forget the beating of... 'battle of bulge'!
Fitness is good, it does keeps one trim:
It is your choice; how to, in life swim!

Tears of euphoria are simply part:
...This of climax, greatest expression of human heart!
We all have laughed, cried a tear:
I have had millions a laugh, which is why I am here!

# STOLEN MOMENTS

A moment, even stolen in time:
That kiss, the act, was perfect rhyme!
When we cuddled, for that first time:
Life where freemium did rhyme!

That was our first caress:
Tantalising, our undress!
But now, I unitise:
Wait is for… truth to realise!

Away from pull, for known what is next:
Trust… this about how you respect!
Just touching for now, nothing more:
In time, future is there to explore!

You are a temple, I will honour:
Our first union, we both shall ponder!
Talk first, as to what each want:
True euphoria… thirst awaits to font!

# STOLEN

This was my car, from outside of house:
The cheese, taken by that illusive mouse!
Things stolen; thieves are in the many:
They take, never give, even a penny!

My wife went missing, I thought how lucky I am:
Then I thought of children, in corner was pram!
Mouths started yelling; but in truth, in life I won:
But then wife returned, exclaimed "shopping done"!

Kids of course, went through ten a bag:
Always a treat, but always nag!
"But I wanted the red one", then the cry:
Stolen for a moment… reason of why!

Tantrum, this as child runs away:
"Ice cream anyone", back they come to stay!
Stolen moments that are part of life:
Thieves are there, but these are like precious time with wife!

# RANDOM CHANCES

Chances are random, they do not occur all day:
They must be taken; or will slip away!
Turning point, where current living changes:
A time for life, where rearranges!

Spin of bottle, during game of 'who goes next':
Game of not knowing, whilst played is 'random text'!
Outcomes are myriad, bring laugh, or something new:
Chance the medium of what will do!

The greatest final guess, none should play against that:
'Game of death', if played… participant needs a real chat!
Randomness is a virtue; thousands take positive road:
Life transformation, or just another story told!

Privilege, this can promote past the random game:
Even with; life can be just the same!
Morality is the factor of, which road to be travelled:
Despair result; if very being, is unraveled!

# EMPOWERED

A new direction, in life to follow:
Not today but starting tomorrow!
Within dreamscape inspiration aroused:
Tantalising ideas that could be empowered!

…Not could; should, see the light of day:
It is me that must initialize their play!
Likened to bird nest, fledglings need to fly:
Activation of… one can but try!

Months have flown, this since first tentative step:
Forming is the outcome, but more time needed yet!
Dough has been rounded, baking still to go:
Now in oven, raising seems so slow!

Baked, now risen into book, workings have now fledged:
Within humour has been wedged!
Feelings of joy to the multitude bring:
My words chorused, hoped not had their final sing!

# CONFIDENTS ALWAYS

Yesterday was a surprise:
As of; what you told me, I was so maximised!
Thought was friends, simply that:
Now… this is a new chat!

But our relationship has never been sensual:
Cuddle, laugh, simply part; we rejoice in conceptual!
I love you, always never in company been sad:
But there is love… type we never will have?

That road is a colder sack:
You are my everything, but not like that!
Impossible for me, is to pass that line:
Kisses yes, but never can we become as fine wine!

Friendship is so often the needed theme:
Between us this the only thing!
With you I laugh, so often truly smile:
You are the mirror of my style!

Respect... this is out trust:
From others, there is never enough!
Two beings, united as if one:
You are the beater, I the gong!

...But now, you ask for more:
This avenue, I cannot explore!
Confidents I hope always to be:
This the path, for you and me!

# MIS-PLACED

Mis-placed again, this my brain:
So often; no thought, as tiredness always does reign!
Wanted is 'REM' sleep… there is so little of that:
Sometimes I full deep, but only after boring chat!

Days of drudgery, we all have them:
Pleasantries are hoped for… emotions they can truly tame!
Evoke real smile, interlude an uninspiring life while:
Bring about much anew, even a change lifestyle!

Life is about the living of… we should, if possible, embrace:
…If we could, all should live in grace!
Any line for true freedom, all join in haste:
Pleasure from the uniformity that is… taste!

Writing… this helps, my eyes do close:
But then another thought, penned ideas can bloom like rose!
Eventually sleep, brings draw of day:
In the morrow, thoughts can again fly away!

# A SMALL FORTUNE

Opulence… Fifty pence to spend on anything I want:
Such luxury, where is the nearest font?
Baffled by choice, with what should I do?
A pending question, if only I had answer too!

Perhaps something sweet, maybe a chocolate bar:
A deposit upon a toy car!
Cigarette… bought, not borrowed from friend:
…Or cup of charr, sugared to buck the trend!

Possibilities few, I might just keep:
Wealth little, but mine… I could weep!
Fifty pence may not be a lot:
But it is all that I have got!

Needed is nothing… decision is to throw away:
Upon path so another might say!
"Mummy, mummy… I am rich":
This before playing in another mud ditch!

# LIES

Seldom, so seldom, any a lie told:
This a family of honesty, where grows no mould!
Truth the essence of what is each's life:
Honesty, this the best way to thrive!

White lies, these may be a fact:
They can help, ease any a real chat!
…If only with family, we could survive:
But others are needed, for us to be alive!

The world is there for all to explore:
Innocence, as part of… can be no more!
Lies creep, they become part of day:
They are simply part, this of the human way!

But this family, even when apart:
From values, do not depart!
Honesty of up-bringing, kids learnt well:
Living in truth… this is the true spell!

# POINT OF NO-RETURN

At point of no-return, this different for each:
Possibilities unlimited… many learn, others teach!
In life, route travelled is ours alone:
Aspirations the determiner of how far thrown!

Looking back upon what was achieved, all can do:
Need always, for that something new!
Failed, or succeeded, we have those memories:
But always, there is the hope for what could be possibilities!

Future is… everyone should fully explore:
We all need, even if this is nothing more!
Reach we can, this to touch the sky:
But by exploring… this is how we get high!

Point of no-return, is when we truly convict:
Make that decision, that too we commit!
Life is… full of consequence:
Sometimes joy… perhaps recompense!

# PRIME TIMES

Moments cherished; these form part of prime time:
End of long day, climax of... a sipped fine wine!
That series that makes your day:
Cream that takes any bitterness away!

...In life, times are few, usually fare apart:
Unexpected occurrences, which touch one's heart!
Could be cloud, gently drifting in sky:
Emotions evoked, even if not known why?

That shower in Summer, that during Winter from you shy:
The burning of yeaning, as tear falls from eye!
To each their own, moments too in thrive:
Times when you know you are truly alive!

That favoured song, that to you always sing:
The moment of placing, of that special ring!
Nights...we have, we sleep to get through:
Moments, even if stolen are precious,
reminiscence of... old and new!

# STRATEGY

Strategy is the planning behind the upcoming new:
Myriad situations that need to be powered through!
Real choice is really in governmental hands:
Most follow rules where democracy stands!

At company level it is just the same:
No lower personnel in the strategic game!
It is true that those at top should know best:
But without listening, companies do become bereft!

At personal level, this point of us:
Decisions made our convictions trust!
Hope is silver lining never rust:
In life strategize we must!

If right; choice can bring great gain:
If wrong be causer of saddest of pain!
Strategy is always part of the human condition:
Winners, and losers, we all have our position!

# WALKING ON AIR

Exhilarating, this the emotion of being right there:
...Of life; no hardships, for a time do you care!
That moment, when achieved is the near impossible dream:
True break from endless constant theme!

First caress of that someone new:
Full-throttled commitment, instead of just getting through!
Release of endorphins that result in flush:
Even cherished event to which you rush!

'Walking on air'; this is the greatest high of all:
Elixir that allows for life; stand or fall!
No tightrope, no need... you can fly:
Lightning is the brain, overwhelmed you laugh, and cry!

Herding thunder of hooves, cacophony cannot compare:
This to elation when you are there!
Endless are aspirations, and dreams:
Simply being is coloured by themes!

# EMPTY PLATE

As child was told; "you must empty your plate":
This prompted a time of create!
But in truth, the taste was only sometimes great:
Out of twenty, would rate less than an eight!

'Spaghetti bolognaise'... this always led to plate being cleared:
Vegetable only brought forth distain... but was how reared!
If plate not emptied got given again:
Belly soon demanded eating, due to hunger pain!

Now adult I have my choice:
Always heard' that of past voice!
Difference now is, always left is that little bit:
My deviance against them times of non-wit!

Bolognaise, or best curry, always left that last mouthful:
It is impossible to finish it all!
Tarnished by parentage, others do understand:
Powerless as child, but now grown human man!

# JIGSAW PUZZLE

Usually two-dimensional, sometimes three:
Complexity is how thousand pieces, and pattern there be!
Like life, can take a long time to complete:
This if you manage to finish... make image neat!

If same colour throughout, then this can be exceedingly difficult:
But what pleasure, this if built!
Time set aside for pieces unity:
Sometimes this seems like, an eternity!

This is part of what is termed' 'leisure time'.
Hours, or days, help from others usually fine!
It is the process that brings about that smile:
Even with help from picture included, itched head for while!

The puzzle can also be riddle of life:
Not only one way to finite, but always strife!
Completion of this is much harder to do:
But with help do get through!

# MY BIRD

My bird is gone, now flown away:
known is that in nature, for long not stay!
Predators too many, combined with no outside knowledge:
This if not return, his last voyage!

Cage outside, hope him to spot:
Decide this home… house bird lot!
Hope is fading, for this is second day:
Sky always onlooking, only hope joy of last sway!

My fault, for my guard was astray:
I allowed little hands, for window to open this day!
Bird was out, within the forbidden room:
But not locked, it had to happen… but not so soon!

Captivity… this can never truly be how life should be:
But for hundreds, rooms are all they see!
Cockatiel by nature, this bird was part of my living day:
Dis-heartened, for no more shall I pay!

# FRIENDS

We all have, at lease I hope:
With their influence, we do cope!
Doses of reality will trend:
Maybe toast, life to end!

People uniting … this is the best:
Unity… this the ultimate caress
That few are there for you:
With friend's life is true!

billion a trail, life going through:
My friends, I know are true!
Between us, we live right:
Hope our friendships do not see night!

Argument's thousands, sometimes go through:
But these, only few!
Even of best of friends have such:
Achieved is little, but this is much!

# CONSIDERATION

Here before anyone, but others want to be first:
...Or that cue dodger, what is the worst?
Perhaps even, someone that will not correct their mistake:
...Or foul attitude, that when passing; others create!

No consideration, this for the simple things in life:
Wave, handshake, or smile, gestures that
cut through sorrow like knife!
When in a bad place, consideration is what you need:
Another doing the washing up, a simple good deed!

Not getting so close, that you can feel another's breath upon neck:
Quiet time, which without consideration, other does wreck!
Being criticised, for what choices you see as best!
...Or being jeered, for saying what is upon your chest!

Non care of children, you are there for them to bend:
...Of partner, only odd 'air hand kiss' to trend!
One moment where appreciation is shown:
You know, grind is not done alone!

# DIS-FUNCTIONAL

When something's not working, times are poor:
Anger surfaces, under threat is that door!
Essence of life is... things will go wrong:
All will at points, hit that gong!

When at low, it is the conjury of what to do?
Mend that thing broken... or replace by new!
Cost is the issue, what is there to pay?
What money will it take to ease anger away?

Perhaps that thing works, but has gone off song:
Computer maybe, messing up even though on!
Dis-functional can be anything at all:
Usually that something small!

...If relationship, then this is awfully bad:
When not smiles, this incredibly sad!
Two opposites can react as if one:
Dis-functionality is simply part of nature's song!

# CHESS

One of the world's most strategic, and cunning of game:
Defeat certainly, or no draw, the ultimate aim!
Pieces each sixteen to plan attack:
Human, or mechanical, experts have their unique knack!

Military precision upon which sacrifices to make:
Ability of part, dependent upon what, given, or take!
Tournaments hundreds, only best make the grade:
To the true masters, reverence must be paid!

Within sphere, great respect of intelligence should be made:
I try, but often a king laid!
Certain strategies even have their own name:
First to be recognised, for contribution to game!

FIDE rated highest, Aagaard, Abasov, to honour but two:
Players with matches still to get through!
The majority do not care about chess:
But for those that play, it is the ultimate process!

# THE WATCHED CLOCK

The watched clock ticks by so slow:
Endlessly around, and around the hands go!
...If one moment you could steal:
You would; to hurry what is to be real!

The result of that pregnancy test?
Paternity known, at last doubt put to rest.
Doctor's analysis, of that which you have held breath?
Perhaps hope again, of what you had been bereft?

Bad feelings that just will not go away:
Apprehension of what might be the coming day!
Each have own problems to get through:
Even the watching for anything new!

Watched clock, could be for the little thing:
Awaiting time for chime to ring!
That which has to be cooked right:
...Or decision when time is so tight!

Progress on standby, that needs that final push:
Ball to fall, as it runs along final cushion'!
Such is… time governs all:
Not matter wherever in life; short, or tall!

Complicated is this world, where all watch the clock:
Traditionally late for that occasion, where so many flock!
Even if last, you may have your go first:
The game that is life is about your thirst!

# MY TRUE LOVE

Sun of day, moon, stars of clear night:
Nothing in nature compares to your insight!
You correct when I am wrong:
Excite, when you wear that throng!

My heart I have given away, but soul this stay:
Debts, have no care… somehow, I will pay!
Your physical form is brilliant for me:
Perhaps our union be remembered in history!

Always smiles, never is there a frown:
To me you are royalty, you wear that crown!
Without… of life I would not cope:
Falter constantly from the slippery slope!

With, I am all that can be:
The sweetest notes that are tranquillity!
Your very being is all I need:
During brevity of life, you are the seed!

# LAST ORDERS

At bar… night was full of cheer:
Talked, laughed so much… but not sure of where was here?
Drinking does make one's brain lame:
But by end of night… that is the game!

Maybe a pickup, but so often not:
But what one can do until morning… is not a lot!
We dream that we are gods in bed:
… In truth, woman walk away, exclaim why? instead!

Humanity is never perfect; we are whom we are:
Each an individual… but in youth, not known true fire!
When young, passions enrage much more:
When married, such can be part of floor!

Alcohol is not for all, but part of life for the majority:
The public house, this the bastille of perhaps a penny!
Release from drudgery… we need this in life:
We need moments free from strife!

# THAT COMPETITION

Progress little, but nearer towards that ultimate goal:
Shortening feature list but taking their toll!
Hope is play, never dull:
But onward, onwards your team does roll!

Others in jubilation continue upon quest:
Grail that is trophy, revered higher than wave crest!
Any surfer's realisation of when life at best:
Forgotten for an instant the world, beating hard your chest!

During knockout competition, teams go home:
Fans supported, but now mourn no throne!
Those that continue, now life is not like gnome:
Apex of game, you enter that final dome!

Waves that are emotions, wash over during game:
Oceans of same colour, up, down, up, down, again, and again!
Vibrating to the rhythm, injuries cause pain:
Your team has prevailed, made all others look tame!

Now in victorious chorus, tears, sweat, singing aloud:
Players of your affection, clap to the crowd!
In sky, noticed not heaviest of cloud:
Pure emotion… of team, you are so proud!

New celebrations now, these as you with others play:
Rejoice in ecstasy, the highlights of this cherished day!
Hugs, and kisses, but also high bill to pay:
Does not matter, your team won… there's simply too much to say!

# TRUE ESSENCE

The fox nose twitched, this as it smelled the air:
This place had dangers, within urban environment were there!
Known was this journey, no further would be home:
Range of territories, only through familiarities did roam!

Within the rural, less dangers for the likes of he:
Could really hide, humans do not see!
But here was urban, he needed to forage to feed:
This not chosen place... but braved, such is need!

Habitats eroded by humans as they encroach upon:
Furry critters joining us... this for their life to go on!
In considering; as humans, we must have a working plan:
We need nature, given up of should never be a gramme!

Upon fox route, one human did shine:
One dog frequented home, this was Betty's shrine!
A kind and gentle hand, that in nature, so many did feed:
...Of humankind was flower, never any weed!

This my mother, remembered in heart:
Our mum was there from our very start!
When needed; mum was always there:
Gone now, but family is everywhere!

# THE BEAST OF TIPSY MOOR

The Beast awaits within shadow for the few:
Grapples in night of those who knew!
Raging fire that erupts from the bellows:
Within influence of bedfellows!

Bottle level lowering, eyes of Beast again do glare:
Beaming through darkness vale, again are there!
Echoes of previous night, now burn true:
Demon that is past comfort limit, steamed through!

Such is life, all want that little more:
...If money there, why not the bottle to further explore?
Evils of brew, do not affect all in same way:
I for one sleep, as bottle draws to end of its day!

With company, raised voices as glasses cheered:
Smiles radiate, this as drinkers are reared!
Frolics of late, an essence of the human aim:
Our species needs stimulus to complete its game!

...If can, so many will alcohol choose:
This to rejoice or forget that news!
Banter is wanted, this is life:
Moments where embraced only stupid strife!

Beasts shall appear, eyes pierce night:
Moments when started is a fight!
Triumph, is where without incident all get through:
No ambulance, or police for work to do!

# ARGUMENTS

They occur, usually over nothing at all:
Next day might shake hands, exclaim "I am the fool"!
Something perceived as wrong... tempers boil:
When really heated, end in broil!

Friends, or enemies... all the same:
But without... humanity loses, arguments can be a gain!
Relationships can only flourish by bouts of truth:
Staying together... this is the ultimate proof!

Lies are exposed, much grovelling usually done:
But at end of day... truth won!
If are meant to be together... will be:
Quarrels are part of life, and history!

...If just an enemy, that argument was just another day:
With friend, relationship end... or simply, go away!
Only truth of living, is arguments will be forever more:
...It is when countries argue, we want this never again to explore!

# PILLOWS

Pillows are the comforters of night, and day:
Weary head of tiredness, or for play!
Head to bury, this as for sleep we strive:
…Or refreshment from awakenment, to provide!

Tucked with cover, this usually same as bed:
Quilt set a bedmate; this must be said!
Never washed, as this ruins their shape:
Replaced through time, refreshed must be comfort scape!

They stay within 'room of night'…spend quiet their day:
Only used when biological does play!
No life, as created by human's they be:
Never really mentioned, importance throughout history!

During bad times they can be a friend:
Cried into when enduring sad trend!
Cuddled into body when life seems at an end:
Water like consistency, they will never bend!

# THE TIPPING POINT

The tipping point is which no one should visit:
Towards never be complicit!
Billions never know their tipping point:
Others towards think of as their anoint!

Living life in safety, the majority do:
Without taking a chance billions get through:
It is those that do chance that earn the big pay:
But so often careless upon their way!

Procedures abandoned so can be earned the big busks:
Attention to the detail, no matter much!
Production is about keeping the costs down:
Skipping safety checks, thousands wear that crown!

The biggest reason for company failure, are the practices within:
Greed of the top, huge profits taken with a grin:
Tipping point breached, life can literally be at an end:
...Or in prison where they tens of dubious friend!

# FRESH WATER

From highest mountain, water begins to trickle:
Snow once, but now not as powdered pickle!
Melting as sunlight does beam:
Little estuaries, that flow to stream!

Lower now, the mountains are no more:
Estuaries become streams, so much life does explore!
The essence of living, this is water without salt:
Biological being of fresh, the result!

Rivers now as fish seems to simply appear:
Land flattening, quantiles of species here!
Bio-matter all does often frequent:
The elixir of life seems to be, from heaven sent!

Now torrents, white in places due to effervescent flow:
Complex in diversity; water is both… fast, and slow!
Purified, this very thing flows from tap:
Coffee, or tea in morning… first taste of that!

# BEGINNINGS

The seed of life marks the first step:
Reproduction, not repetition, the most vital concept!
Growth the measure, of can a species survive.
Territory the factor as to will bio-form thrive!

We have vast solutions to humanities ongoing storm:
But neglect, dwindling numbers of other species born!
Science has progressed further than we could have dreamed:
Now it is time for a united theme!

All countries, including those that are wealth poor:
Must protect nature, simply do more!
The gulf between the wealthy, or those with little is vast:
But a blanket around all bio form must be cast!

Resources must be given, but not for the in-power aid:
Debt of humanity to nature, this must be paid!
Given randomly to governments, this should be no more:
Where influx needed, this the true explore!

If you become rice because of job, well done:
Exploitation, this should not be spun!
Taking from the cookie jar, this is wrong:
Might be open, but not just for one!

Beginning is truth of path:
But if not cure, humanity may not last!
Billions support the idea that we should support our bio-dome:
But millions, they simply stay at home!

# THE SUN TO CHEER

Rain, rain, rain… this has been May:
I have gardening to do, but in garden cannot play!
So many weeds, as my green fades:
Where do they come from… 'all my days'?

Only risking showers, walkies I can do:
Shorter walks…but for babies, must bare through!
Want is… for sun to again shine:
Clouds to disappear… day to be a fine wine!

At last tasted, is the purity of this weather brew:
Not a cloud, sun beaming… true!
Longer walks, plus chores of outside can be done:
Time again for fun!

Mown, the yellows are no more:
Green is that which I adore!
Now sat with glass in hand:
For such smugness might pay a grand!

# FORGOTTEN PROMISES

Promises made in youth:
For moments of passion past the truth!
We all lie, white to keep things sweet:
Black is wrong, offer only deceit!

For protection of those whom we love:
Ask that, which might be above!
Family is our union, is what makes a heart truly sing:
Without, in truth… there is nothing!

Questions asked by little ones, you cannot face yet:
Gooseberry buss, for now… they can accept!
Maybe cabbage patch, they go to investigate:
Running, is baby there… imagination is so great!

…But black lies, these are wrong:
Constantly form part of humanity's song!
Implicate others into… in nefarious scheme:
Wanted not, but in life, an ongoing theme!

# PROMISES AND LIES

A promise made in youth:
For moments of passion past the truth!
We all lie, white to keep things sweet:
Black is wrong, offer only deceit!

For protection of those whom we love:
Ask majesty of the above!
Family is our union, is what makes a heart truly sing:
Without, in truth... there is nothing!

Questions asked by little ones, you cannot face yet:
Gooseberry bush, for now... they can accept!
Maybe cabbage patch, they go to investigate:
Running, "is baby there"? imagination is so great!

But black lies, these are wrong:
Constantly form part of humanity's song!
Implicate others into... in nefarious scheme:
Wanted not, but in life, an ongoing theme!

Promises, even made in lie, should be kept:
You cannot promise, then deny a pet!
A lie is a lie, for the most we do regret:
It is the white, we all do forget!

Lies by nature, seem to be wrong:
Hundreds smell the bad, must distaste their pong!
Through promises made we all go on:
Only upon death bed, from life are they gone!

# MY RUSTY NAIL

Bench once so sturdy, now so old:
Simply friend of memorable stories told!
Garden adornment of memories now faded:
But known when sat upon, important talks persuaded!

This year my mate did collapse:
Punished by time now had enough of that!
Nails of frame were nearly all bent brown:
But one still solid, demanded a new crown!

Not much to see, but had supported family for so long:
Buffed back to perfection, its importance would continue on!
But in what? there was no real choice:
A bench part again, this would be nail voice!

The inanimate, it is true such cannot sing:
But in life small can be the needed thing!
Recycling, if possible, there should be enemy:
This nail now is for support of new generations of family!

# CRY OF NATURE

Willows wept as Mother again cried:
Polices let down, only partial begging did provide!
Humanity yet to get, we need nature as our friend:
...If wanted global warming to put to an end!

Now the time is to start denying our neglect:
But through increasing population, can never truly correct!
Children's future, this must be put first:
Yet due to monetary concerns, there is little thirst!

Weeping willow is a place from rain to hide:
Below canopy white, temporary protection provide!
Nature offers barrier few:
In defence of value ideas must be new!

All currently shelter from the storms to come:
Environmental disaster effects everyone!
Not known is the turmoil that shall be:
But truly, one day, be marked by history!

# CHOICES

Wanted was sandwich of ham, with strawberry jam:
...But then he is only six!
I love ham but with pickle, that I can cram:
Choices can be strange of what we do mix!

That something strange that is put upon toast:
...Or oddest thing that you add to Sunday roast!
Certain combinations work for the populous most:
Laugh we do at what eaters of weird post!

Banana and bacon, might be that what you fix:
Test of anything, to which you ram!
Randomness is that all have own pick:
That eaten as you push first pram!

Life is living, do not do as the rest:
Be individual, in that you are the best!
...If choices are all, that is humanity:
Make this for you, never any other human that be!

# EQUALITY

From animosity, I will not turn my head:
I though not strong, will fight against instead!
My body, this too week for physical fight be:
But stand against of course, any atrocity!

The weak need the strong, this to continue on:
Wiped out if compassion is not, the human song!
World's nations must have true interest:
Acting for equality... this should be where priorities rest!

Margined groups have the right for voice to be heard:
Not insulted via decisions that appear as absurd!
In street... if someone collapses, ten's will gather to give aid:
Compassion... the trait to which highest reverence paid!

Groups are manyfold, come in all sizes, and forms:
Most have little garden, hundred's large lawns!
Never can be the gaps of, 'living standard' equalised:
But through global concerns, future generations may be surprised!

# TENTATIVE STEPS

...It is that first step, taken in new direction:
Earliest footfall... this that measure of life correction!
Tentative for now, as long path ahead:
Trodden before by hundred's, only true knowledge... words said!

Braving the new wild, footprints covered a mile:
Stepped with enthusiasm, for this was Mary's style!
Needed was a journey; another course follow, to end:
Completed were thousand's, but this would
become Mary's best friend!

Her quest, to prove if opinions held were right:
Passage of discovery, continue through day, and night!
Questions her footage, even if head lain low:
This was Mary's life, the truth she had to know!

Arguments, and cuddles, smiles, and odd frown:
Husband, and wife, had battled through night; both had grown!
The choice had finally seen the light:
Bed Mary had chosen, this would be their comforter of night!

Throughout weeks before, hundreds of shops they did explore:
None seemed to have been just what either did adore!
Decision came down to only three things:
Comfort, and price, plus fact of marriage... wife always wins!

To get your dream, you must give your pay:
Moments when the wife can swoon away!
By giving in; you in fact, did also that battle win:
...Of wife's happiness, inside you wear the 'contentment pin'!

Future shall bring, other opportunities to debate:
...If reasoned right, your relationship can be great!
Life is about choices after all:
Do you walk stumbling, or tall?

# LEVERAGE

Leverage is... having the power to take, or put right:
Give solution to problems, most hidden from sight!
Having the advantage, that you know
problems you can get through:
Have ability that hardship will not affect you!

Use resources, that to others can be bold!
Influence decisions, because of secrets you were told!
Having the power, that you can control:
Those that have the true petrol!

Manipulation: that is the name of the game:
Money the reason... this for achieving aim!
Those at top know the game best:
There's is, how life they caress!

Insidious... this is the life the worst of us do rule:
Maybe gang, but also as governments tool!
Our liberty taken, this to make the millions so rich:
The poor always to end up in ditch!

# Phased in mind

Clouds of mind appear, this as alcohol goes down:
No fear for body, this as in euphoria you drown!
Public occasion, this the place usually be:
Moments that sometimes remain in your history!

Quite often forgotten the night before:
Your behaviour, that from others you would deplore!
Now awake, you think 'what happened last night'?
Lucky if no bruises, these from stupid fight:

In slumber, your head still a mess:
Your true needs, you do not address!
Now is recovery, from the night before:
As time passes, you become again much more!

Night again looms, but this time you do not play:
Known is... there is other a day!
Money of course dose play its ...part
If consequences, it is because you did start!

# TRIFLING MATTERS

Trifling matters are those that irritate, not real problems create:
Niggling concerns that have to be addressed, these too appreciate!
millions confront, others want to go away:
There for all, dream of night, or passage of day!

Perhaps, payment for something that you forgot:
Someone reminding, this of thing you did not!
Forgotten that food, that in cupboard is rotting fast:
Flies the indicator, body into action must blast!

Tablets not taken, this due to other concerns:
Making sure you have the information, as your child learns!
Correcting that problem that in innocence you did create:
Again, repeating an action, you must replicate!

Trifling matters may make you scratch your head:
Solutions too, you may need your bed!
As time endures, the mind loses its clarity:
Absence of thought, part of life that be!

# INSURANCE

The millions have insurance, but there is always a deductible:
That amount in claim, we are not fool!
...If car, not worth that claim:
Premiums being lowed, the real aim!

One discretion of policy, all can go wrong:
Fifty pound added to your monthly song!
So, we claim if car, only when wrecked:
Then we find; criminality comes next!

You might get hit by another, with no insurance at all:
...And so, only in debt you fall!
Insurance is a demon, so often in 'sheep's clothing' disguised:
It is when claim made, you are genuinely surprised!

Within the small print, that which no one does read:
Clauses, unfair... but the providers viewed them as a need!
The purpose for the insurance, in fact was not covered at all:
You paid the premiums, now are enraged... feel so small!

# MORAL FIBRE

Moral backbone to stand, or wings of flight:
Disappearing quickly, from what might be plight!
Usually later, as self-preservation is human right:
Hostility is best left; all enjoy comfortable night!

Standing against criminal behaviour, this is entirely another thing:
Within decent society, we report what is seen!
Intervene one or three do, quite often it just takes a shout:
Most criminals are cowards, rapidly vacating scene, they bug out!

Perhaps stance for cause, you view something as wrong:
…So, you join the chorus, of that life song!
Bringing justice… if you do your moral fibre is good:
Your heart is certainly not made from wood!

Trying to right wrong's, I wish we all would do:
Those that cause problems, they are the few!
Life would be fantastic; this if there were no problems, or crime:
But known is… atrocities occur all the time!

# HITTING THE HIGH NOTES

Not as a singer, only a unique few can do that:
Not as a surgeon, their ability… better than best acrobat!
Believed is that all have uniqueness… this to hit the high:
But in what sphere, may any of us fly?

Not be trained from day dot… to achieve:
Not pressured by parenting, to fulfil their perceive!
Realised the fact; that you are better than anybody you know:
This that thing; high notes of touch, this as during life you go!

Climax is… when you reach highest peak of sphere:
…If Olympian, gold medal bring, true tear!
Upon receiving, joined by billions as they also cry:
'Joy of heart', you they do provide!

Sport, science, literature, music, fields vast; for common cause:
The greatest within, receive the loudest applause!
Each generation has within it, so much cream:
Cherry upon top… this is the goal, the dream!

# BREWING TIME

Got the fruit, now other bits to order:
Picking of stems, hundreds on choice boarder!
Already day two grapes are within my sleep:
Red, and white, chosen fruit all so sweet!

Within mouth goes so much:
Excuse tasting, this to improve the final clutch!
Three days later, all fruit strained, and gone:
Liquid only, the brewing process can go on!

Added the ingredients, begins now the brew:
In week's, this liquor will be something new!
The aromas through the airlock are fine:
Temperature right, but still long time before wine!

Now time to clear, fermentation complete:
Bubbling has stopped, only bottling process to make neat!
Time the giver, of a thing new:
Only hope this time, made was something true!

# VALUE

Everything has a value high, or low:
Quality the determiner of; highest museums they show!
Lowest priced are most common of things:
Candle, pencil, or paper, little objects, but with heart sings!

It is the value of 'Mother nature', that has the highest price:
True conviction to aid would be nice!
Economies rich, can certainly do their bit:
Will they truly, the majority have that itch!

Companies ravish resources for profit, this will continue:
Legal, or illegal red tape covers every avenue!
If activities challenged, courts take far too long to decide:
Are their processes worth what they provide?

Life itself has another value, though millions have no care:
They destroy, this because they dare!
Consequences if caught, but they are willing to take that chance:
Live do thousands in total elegance!

# INSIDIOUS

Insidious are those which cause mayhem in life:
Only aim, to cause as many others as possible strife!
Usually sitting in anonymity:
Intention only to reap havoc, wreck community!

Not own, for these interrupters smile as they play:
Smile, even if for money, this not that day!
Complicating an individual's way:
All they want, is for others to pay!

Insidious intruders, computer their chosen tool:
Code they know, none of computing are fool!
Dismantling fabric of our society:
But only path taken, that of criminality!

Invaders of privacy, they terrorise in pack, or alone:
Operate from locations that are never known!
Increasingly sophisticated, are their cunning strategies:
Until caught, only themselves do they please!

# ELEVATION

Within the urban cranes stand tall:
Tower above us all!
Only highest building, you look down upon:
Lifters of the industrial, they are urbanisations song!

When development new, their presence is felt:
Blocked roads make your patients melt!
Looking up you see heavy loads swinging free:
Fluorescent yellows worn area is dangerous, you know that's true!

Who would brave work high in sky?
This thought of thousands as they venture by!
Paid well yes, but what a job to do:
Reverence given to those little few!

Lifts that can take to top of tower:
Confined space for minutes, or steps that take hour!
Upon flat the majority do remain:
Away from urban where life very tame!

# OMINOUS

Those clouds are filling the sky:
Black: heavy laden, soon Earth will see their provide!
Inside now, so bring on this rain:
Not too much, because I want garden again!

Refreshing my green, and flowers… in this I pride:
Time now is my only guide!
Nature replenishes, give what we really need:
Supplies the bio-forms, sustenance indeed!

For now, the sky is dark:
This before the torrent, that soon will embark!
But will come, the warmth of sun once more:
Guaranteed, another day to explore!

Now refreshed from slumber, sunshine my eyes do greet:
I smile as arise to feet!
New day brings with it, so much potentially:
Time will show, this if it favours me!

# THAT 'FEELING OF KNOWING'

Being in a place you have never been:
But remembering as if home scene!
Maybe smells, colours, or structures, mix of the three:
Within be tingling sensation that effects thee!

Your essence senses, knows you have been here before:
But as for remembrance of, there is nothing more!
In you take a deep breath, closed are your eyes:
Now time for ponderance, you never know what could surprise!

Standing you suddenly shudder, an image before your eyes:
Truth, or not, clarity begins to unwind!
Small increments first, but then bubble can burst:
Memory now amongst your worst!

...So long ago betrayed by a friend:
This was that place, where your relationship did end!
Forgotten as child, for family had moved long ago:
Though now the first friend with affection did know!

# CURTAINS DRAWN

Brightest of days, but curtains are closed tight:
Television is on, so refraction is not as bright!
Clothing not needed; I am on my own:
Shower only warm, feels like a thrown!

Under flowing water, majesty is as… skin it cools:
Time of luxury, dogs also want under… they no fools!
Towel not even needed; your skin is quickly 'heat dried':
Thoughts of a second later, the extra comfort it will provide!

So hot, outside you cannot sit, or lay:
If shut your eyes, later will with pain pay!
Odd wonderings, yes these can be made:
No dog walking, as under conditions… they will fade!

Water plentiful, fan if available to cool down:
Warmth is a joy, extreme heat upon we frown!
Natural warmth is the best when outside:
…If extreme; it is up to you to decide!

# Winds of change

Concerned, or not, this the debate this day:
Restriction under with we have coped… blown away!
Baking hot, but there is still a constant breeze:
Apprehension if… even saw a sneeze!

Sixteen months in; but new decision can easily be reversed:
'Winds of change', these the government's verse!
Sighs of relieve for most; but, what about
the 'immune compromised'?
Partying is good, but others cannot… if to survive!

Cautious should be all, this virus is not done yet:
…But wave of pleasure has caressed so many young!
Face coverings still, these in packed areas of life:
Time will show if dropping restrictions decision Is right!

Within democracy; we the people should be free:
Open again is our economy!
Doubted is another hurricane, but perhaps stern wind:
Only hope humanity learn, respect this win!

# SMALL FRY

When in a pond you cannot swim to another:
...Must be carried if placed other!
Big fish or small home is home:
Within your boundaries have freedom to roam!

I live in shallows of small pond; this is my territory:
Mouths have been seen, that could swallow me!
But those are still far enough away:
Safe is now... but tomorrow is another day!

With a friend I play, I play:
Merriment passes time away, away!
Raining now water droplets swell my pond:
Jeepers, a friend is gobbled... gone!

Mouths are coming, in crevice do I hide:
Shrinking is their distance, divide!
Warmth of sun now, gobblers have gone, gone:
fellow swimmers taken, this feels so wrong, wrong!

Few friends left now; we do still play:
Months have passed since birthing day!
Our shallows now seem so small:
Soon we must leave, sacrifice all!

Mouths are coming, I shut my eyes tight:
Grimace for this is my life's night!
But no, I have not been taken like my friends:
Why know not but flee to pond other ends!

Days pass, still I be:
New wonderments of the deep, happy is me!
Realized now is the fact that I am big... big:
Gobbler I am, that I dig... dig!

# ICE

Ice to humans is a real danger:
But for alcohol, be a true friend!
That cubed, or crushed chill of your chosen:
Without, you could not recommend!

Enhancer, of that drink we greet:
malt perfect, this should be neat!

glaciers are the gigantic structures:
These near polls dominate!
They are the coolers of Earth:
Maintenance of; we must concentrate!

Ice burgs break off; due to warming, float in sea:
Were once true menace to shipping, now are technology seen!

Massive structures of most fresh water:
For singletons they are a profit dream!
Can be towed to safer waters:
There purity of water gleamed!

At highest altitude, ice is always there:
Great danger for climbers, traversing taken great care!

The largest expanse of, this the ice shelves:
Explorers few, have navigated in extreme cold!
Passage of time trapped within its layers:
They are the tellers of our past!

From metal canasters, ice in analysed:
Scientists of climatic changes not surprised!

Within freezers across our planet, melted would be sad:
Ice keeps food from going bad!
Fresh keeps the fish caught at sea:
No delights if iced not be!

... If touched, can cause burn:
Gloves needed, long ago humans did learn!

Spread across vast areas of land zone:
People few choose to make their home!
Eskimos are the best known people that frequent:
Living within domes, there they lament!
The one problem is Wintertime:
Thought of ice feared, danger only chime!

Stalactite, or stalagmite, ice comes in tens of forms:
Temperature key to where it adorns!
Frozen landscapes, are most beautiful of all scenes:
Upon so many a Christmas card, this as snow gleams!

Permafrost: land long frozen, but now thaws:
We cannot keep breaking mother's laws!

# QUICK SNACKS

Cheese on toast with pickle, this is loved the most:
This as one of them quick snacks, which millions post!
Bacon filled roll with lashings of tomato gold!
Thousands a day consume, or so I am told!

Heated soup when stomach not feeling right:
First food of day, cereal that create smiles at sight!
Delicacies of high street, aromas of shops have enticed you in:
Hot patty, or the simplest thing!

A quick snack can be anything at all:
Hot, or cold, eaten with glee that makes one feel tall!
That munch that pleases one so:
Bouncing after consumption, off you go!

Buying these temptation's, we may not have the means:
Mouth waters, but those pleasures in your dreams!
Cheap by their very nature, but even one you cannot afford!
Sigh as head lowered, poor have nothing accept the lord!

# LIFE'S BLOOD

The blood of life, is that which farmers provide:
Arable, or animal; reverence... without humanity does not survive!
Choice to farm, this is commitment to hardest work:
Through all weather's farmers never shirk!

...If arable; crops thousands of farmers must sow:
But first prepare land, this to aid the way they grow!
Planting has short season, harvesting of too:
Profit from labours effort, few farmers do!

...If animal; many a cold morning, an early night:
Braved must be all weathers, upon land rearing must do!
Always observant. Cannot afford to miss any glitch:
Even in this sphere, very few farmers are rich!

Upon sea, boats must return to port with real catch:
Skippers knowledge of best locations, no other match!
Type of fishing, dependent upon what is delivered to shore:
Varying values of fishers can never be sure!

All aspects of farming, are 'lifeblood'… this is a fact:
For so few, they with nature, have made their pact!
The providers of the fresh produce… they deserve real pay:
But like everything in life, few have that day!

Governmental polices; these govern, all that the harvesters do:
Implications that control practices, cost the revered few!
Subsidies yes; these the government do pay:
Charges they should also, this so farmers have time for play!

# BALANCING THE EQUATION

The real question is how, this an equation is balanced?
This when it comes to equality of pay!
Gaps between top, and bottom are increasing:
...If equality, should not this be going the other way?

It is the system that is broken:
But then it has been for so long!
At least there is a minimum wage now:
Legally you are entitled to a working song!

Problem is... poor wages, mean you just get along:
No chance of holiday, luxuries are not your life!
Simply surviving... paying bills that constantly appear:
No scalpel to cut through, only knife!

Sometimes luck comes your way, that extra shift:
...Or pay rise, either give your life a lift!
Those that work in the public sector:
These need a true wage rise to vector!

A real change, in government policy direction:
Inflation continuous; small increments mean, no life correction!
The needed workforce... their potential is there:
...But without the real living opportunity, why should they care?

Society needs to be enriched; it would be if, money earned:
But year after year, no governing body has learned!
Contentment of the population, this has
to become the primary concern:
One day this lesson, employers might learn!

# TRUE POWER

The power of thought, is much stronger than the fist:
Power is... when in multitude directions, you can twist!
Aggression might win fights, especially if pacifist does not resist:
Harm only caused if... hostility does persist!

The antagonistic person might win a day:
But also take beating along their way!
Their ability is that to scare, frighten others... perhaps for pay:
Cause occurrences where hope has become stray!

Yet it is the thinkers, those that have no need to fight:
Those in charge, which collect the greatest payment each night!
The true power, always lays in plain sight:
This is the way of humanity, our species plight!

Sometimes, the heart might rule the head:
Passion flaring for another, mistakes made instead!
Wealth brings power; the world's population knows, that said:
Each have their life, whatever the bed!

# COMMITMENT

Commitment is... when you honour your lover:
You do not cheat with any other!
Days spent; smiling when you think their name:
Devoted, you are lover, friend... they your flame!

That flicker of candle, which cannot be relighted:
Truth of worth... this that is always recited!
Once committed; you do anything to keep, and defend:
Life is about that person, you depend!

...of course, commitment can be to other cause:
Dedication: to that thing you know, will bring you applause!
Recognised activity: that at apex, 'wins the day':
Devotion too; endless preparation, now does pay!

Common goal of... just getting something done:
This night: you will go out, will have with friends... fun!
Myriad: are commitments, but all have same theme:
Must be stuck to, this to achieve that dream!

# The friendship of science

Science is a friend to all:
…Of its importance, effects are never small!
Pen, or paper, science is involved:
Making of… processes scientific are solved!

Tap water has to be cleaned:
Car paint, this must be gleamed!
Wheelchairs and buggies are increasingly made:
Reverence to science behind manufacture must be paid!

Everything we eat, or drink… science is behind it all:
We are cave dwellers if none; humanity would simply fall!
Cutlery with which we eat must be processed:
Through varied applications of… life has progressed!

In classroom, for all it does fill with wonder:
Inquisitive minds questioning, its application ponder!
Advances in techniques will take us where we need:
Science is a true friend indeed!

# IRONY OF LIFE

Infrastructure not built by the best, rather best placed:
Lowest tenders for jobs taken with great haste!
Penalties yes; this if work proves to be shoddy:
Cowboys numerous, like the taste of the 'money lolly'!

Bid will they upon big jobs that need to be done:
Ability is needed, after getting… they have fun!
Cheapest materials used, substandard to the need:
As project continues, you pay increments agreed!

At job completion you pay the outstanding amount:
Impressed with the build; cost for the needed, you count!
Proud you might stand, embrace the new each day:
…But then, you notice something has gone astray!

Concerned; you call the number always answered before:
Now only a discontinued tone, you fall to floor!
Realisation that this job is not what it appeared to be:
Another inspects, tells you the worst… contractor now history!

# THE FALLS

Tranquil ripples of this shallow blue:
Currents leading towards one of mother's true brew!
Greenery varied, aligns the shores:
Fury of natural; this as nature now roars!

Blue transformed to white, as towards falls the river does rage:
Maelstrom of bubbling, this as rocks the river does engage!
Aromas here pungent, tasted is the air:
Mesmerised by the awe of this place, I can but stare!

The barren downs, allow water to cascade:
Thunderous sounds; as here… Earth marvel, Mother does parade!
Mist is everywhere, result of water's plunge:
Memory of place, time can never expunge!

Effervescent white foaming towards lower shore:
Rainbows appear; but are low to new quietening at cliffs floor!
Settling, the waters below convert back to blue:
Flow again in river, rockpools few, highs bottom… appears so new!

# THIRST

Thirst was not for water, rather success:
Making true, and real progress!
Say that during life, at one time "I was the best":
Doing just once, something better than the rest!

Hunger for this time effort to manifest:
Even getting the burden off of your chest!
Now your creation others will caress:
Elation button of you, so many smiles press!

The thirst for new... this humanities greatest song:
True time of individuality is never long!
Time flows as if river, ripples always there:
Chorus of those who changed... fundamentals of which we care!

Good ideas have flourished, are part of modern-day wear:
Enriched the present, where which once there was despair!
Space the next conquest, even though things will go wrong:
Life should be enjoyed, this until it's final gong!

# RECTIFY THAT WHICH IS WRONG

...In unity, we have attachment, togetherness for a cause:
We may need help of others, perhaps simply their applause!
If something needs doing, it might take one to get this done:
Collective at conclusion, better for majority to have won!

...But causes so many, overwhelming numbers get nowhere at all:
Filed as irrelevant, purpose of... only heard by wall!
Those that can remedy, only here own noise:
Play only in box, of their own tools!

Box does open, but only when seen as best thing to do:
Righted are cause, but these so few!
...If company, why change money maker at all?
...If government, same thing guides them as if tall!

Money: greed of, or simply being available for problems to correct:
Those that do protest, they need real voice to direct!
Only pressure, this enforced by those below:
Unity of the people, to rectify wrong's we must show!

# WHY BE SAD

Once inflamed, now ashes:
Past now before eyes dashes!
Nearing moment when life say goodbye:
Body failed, now in sky!

Looking down see those that mourn:
Cannot converse, from life are torn!
With delight, kiss living from the above:
Only felling, that of true love!

Respect shown, upon life you did impact:
Crying at grave, your closest are compact!
Words spoken, honour who you were:
Tears flow, as recited is your owe!

…But a life remembered, is great:
Pictures, videos, from past smiles create!
Above, you see the love you really had:
In death, why be sad?

# SHIFTING IDEAS

Clear, then forgotten, within fleeting second gone:
Through 'bustle of life', are part of humanity's song!
At night within dream, amazement as you do wake:
Again, in slumber, other ideas your noddle does bake!

Remembrance of; so hard, but often written down:
Still as dough, others at might frown!
Cooking in 'oven of thought', unbaked does rise:
Baking with heat, supply great surprise!

Nature of; does not matter, they become your aim:
Baby of; what might be your fame!
Baking done, that idea has fledged:
Word of achievement, money for application pledged!

Pioneering game changer, or personal thing:
Most important, from your brain the now did bring!
Failures are commonplace, to to successes, I say this:
Congratulations… realised is your wish!

# OUR FUTURE TRUTH

…Of futuristic adventures: upon screen we see imagined truth:
But only what is realised, will be the proof!
Interstellar travel, can this ever be achieved?
Through scientific advances, this must be believed!

The internet too many older is so new:
The young simply, something that they work through!
Within thirty years, everything has changed:
Life itself has been totally rearranged!

…Our future, what will it be?
Who knows, what the course of humanity?
Scientific advances, these are what our species need:
Space travel to find resources; never necessary, as final deed!

Perhaps Earth problems, we can correct:
Through endurance… scientific, with nature reconnect!
Make a future, where the majority would respect:
Not this world of dis-connect!

# PERSONAL DATA

Information: this is the true liquid gold:
Fact when buys of privacy do unfold!
Leakages of data, that for you are the 'holy grail':
Criminality used, your very life can dis-rail!

...But it is personal fact, these that aid modern life to run:
'Internet banking', all hope never to be threatened by theft gun!
Trust is everything, in so many companies we have this:
Fraud alerts frighten, known is our world can become an abyss!

The world of online is here, it will always stay:
This is how the most live in the new way!
Even actual money, for advanced individuals this is gone:
Cards have replaced, but is this wrong?

Sealed his fate, this unless catastrophe does strike:
Still for multitude, technology is not within sight!
Few still live, using the simplest of way:
Parted from computing world, they make their hay!

Our species has the ability to manipulate all that be:
Even weather patterns, are affected by the likes of we!
Control of resources is envied, craved by the few:
Heretical structure needed, normal for humanity to follow, to do!

# WAFER THIN

The ultimate competition, is that of the Olympic games:
An occasion of jubilation, or emotional flames!
Torch always burns, the ignition of past:
Flaming standing for; unity, that competitors cast!

The margins were tiny, near nothing at all:
At the top level, there can be no fall!
Only few reach heights; were medals are won:
Not for me, but perhaps another loved one!

The effort an athlete puts in, this to have their day:
Upon performance, nations have their say!
Congratulations to those; that have medal achieved:
Commiseration to those, where performance did not believe!

True humanity is... camaraderie, respect of all other:
Family is not just... biological sister, or brother!
Within communities of democracy, humanity stands tall:
Athletes stand for the competition that is within all!

# THE RADICAL THAT BE

Towards the dis-abled, the seriously do recourse:
Even if joining in, think the worse!
Their disability is, they are not part of this group:
Not cool with a challenged persons personal loop!

Niggled at, fingers pointing, this is their day:
Unfair criticism: for millions in society, this is their way!
Treated like dirt so often are:
Should not even drive a car!

Truth is… any handicap can be a true inspiration of Earth:
Generations before had no time for their worth!
Brain never had its day:
Put away, this is humanity did play!

…But know is a time, where humanity equalised:
Remembered past, but true value be realised!
Special Olympics shows that the world has moved on:
Those that could have died still be part of humanities song!

# CAUTION THE PLAY

Caution the play, not sure of what is going on:
Unknown the contenders, or those that... they you stare upon!
Ability is so often the key, this too if you can defeat any of these:
Knowledge; through observance, your eyes may please!

Caution still the play, others might want to deceive:
Keep back their level of quality, wool of their weave!
Such is nature, this of the gamblers kind:
If win, another could be truly dined!

Big win, life is laughs, life is at its caress:
Money won... this is better than even marriage dress!
Struggling; this is now a time to thrive:
Equalities too now; all you have survived!

But losing; this is the solemn time:
...If partner, no recreational rhyme!
Even objection: this has been talked about of course:
Now alone... life of earlier, end in divorce!

# ATTENTION TO THE DETAIL

Within the big picture, are pixels so small:
Sometime ignored, but attention needed to address all!
Bit-parts; just like us in the pattern that is life:
Value huge for perfection, whole aim to avoid strife!

Within contract; the smallest written lines:
Those inclusions which restrict, ensure issuers fines!
Details are pre-requisites, must be to carry on:
Pain to all, but within contracts notes of song!

Any poorly made item that simply falls apart:
These are cheap, no attention to from production start!
A high-end watch is exact, never misses time:
Detail is what makes any mechanical goods chime!

Any musical scores would be incomplete:
The tallest mountains, climbers would never defeat!
Our very life's are detailed, planned what we do:
These are your choices, your existence, I leave them up to you!

# ROOTS

So seldom seen, the lifeblood of survival itself:
Strong roots are essential for future food wealth!
Even if tragedy does strike, the plant above ground gone:
The roots can resurrect, supply sustenance for life to continue on!

Food shortage of the future, shall become a theme:
But because of scientific advances of agriculture, bell does not ring!
The roots of today's crops are in reality weak:
But it is possible that one day nature even we cheat!

Known is roots have their own biosphere:
...If small area, longevity can never be clear!
Trees for example have roots vast, and strong:
Their existence span can be ever so long!

Fire in nature is a devastating thing:
But because of deep roots, again a tree may again spring!
What would happen if crops were the same?
No ploughing, just harvesting only yearly pain!

No need for seeding, birds consume, loss farmer's pain:
Fewer weather worries, this because of established root gain!
Cutting with harvester becoming the food gathering dream:
Profitable farming becoming the common theme!

Crops that thrive through conditions,
that today cause financial pain:
Faces of the agricultural hero, never by crop failure wain!
Fundamental food sources that are not compromised:
A real degree of satisfaction be realised!

As a species, our population is out of control:
We need science to advance, this if eat from future cherry bowl!
Stagnation of new thinking, this cannot be humanity's path:
We need scientific positivity, this if we at nature can laugh!

Root investigation is the answer, working out the best way to grow:
We already know the big are stable, so
with root knowledge can sow!
Feeding the people, we must adapt if we want to do:
The future we might not see, but descendants they will!

# ETHICS

In trust we live, respect each other:
Honor, and abbey, the rules… loyalty to cause, same as brother!
Pain must be endured, this for fair society:
Goodness of heart is the place to be!

At the end of day, giving cannot be wrong:
But keep your precious… your life must go on!
'Moral fiber' is the measure of all:
…If upstanding, that person shall always walk tall!

Deeds, and efforts, these are definers of morality:
Controlled should not be others, just shown respectability!
…Yes, sometimes we need say nothing too:
A gesture of hello never gets through!

vehicles that race in village, double the limit their choice:
drunken; ignition keys turned, instead of being hoist!
Two examples of reality where morality not there:
Ethics good, this is for what we care!

# SWINGS AND ROUNDABOUTS

Human life is about the swings, and the roundabouts:
Even truths are not clear, there are always doubts!
Our worth is the value we give to humanity:
Offering so much dependent upon one's personality!

Swings stand for changing direction of life:
The highs, and lows, which generate elation, and strife!
One day news that brings smile to face:
The next sorrow, something has happened, slowing heart pace!

Roundabouts depict the circler motion of events:
Time governs there affect upon an individual... how intense!
It is said, "time is the greatest heeler" ... it's deletion:
But seems so short when moments of celebration!

Tears of joy, or sorrow, in life are a constant theme:
Like paper, can come in ream!
Emotions so many will cross all upon living path:
Hoped is... positive shall generate laugh!

# THE LAWN OF DELIGHT

Upon once perfection, weeds did now encroach:
'Labour of love', blemished, eyes tearful… before memories poach!
This garden was a individuals delight:
Bare not could they, this space in light!

Accident had taken, ability to perform task away:
Now from once lawn, absent would stay!
No other could touch, not even see:
Even if ravished by nature, which is how that be!

Purple, white, brown, green, each frequent the never seen:
Lawn obliterated; these colours are the new theme!
But now eyes did not well, but rather gleam:
Healing was the person, soon be realised a distant scheme!

Garden entered, needed equipment in hands:
Brown only colour, nothing within garden now stands!
Seeded, then watered, grass can regrow:
This environ, never again be like hedgerow!

Daily ritual of pride resumed once again:
Known the fact, physical bring great pain!
…But this is a love labour, maintenance will resolve:
Believed must, that fortune favours the bold!

# CHARACTER BUILT

Desolate… not left even crumbs to taste:
Those… the non-invited, eaten all that I did baste!
I invited friend around, thought that might be nice:
But now in future, will always think twice!

Came with others, very few drinks did they bring:
All wanted to be part of house scene!
In truth, parties are not my thing:
…But friendship does make my heart sing!

Waters deep have governed whom I am:
Sure; was not this way from pram!
Caused by life experience, this must be the truth:
Perhaps how treated when in youth?

Quiet life, which is wanted, who I be:
Want only friends that believe in me!
Maybe party, but only small crowd:
Need to meet, or always within shroud!

# TRUST OF THE SYSTEM

A law is passed, we make our feelings felt:
Emotionally thrive, or simply melt!
Elation, or condemnation, once written are law of that land:
If in deviance, officers may upon door pound!

Just society: we all know the world offers not:
Even within the democratic, finances rule the lot!
Long before birth law can decide fate:
The system is rigged, this for profits to generate!

The mighty do fall, but seldom is there a Samson:
Humanity by the powerful is always held to ransom!
We do compete, but so often the playing field is not fair:
Known by the elite, justice will never be there!

This elite are not all those with real money:
Thousands have earnt wealth, are kind good as honey!
But when it comes to business, find the proof:
Corruption is rife, we all know this is the world's truth!

# MYSTERY OF THE WOODS

The woods were feared, stories of told:
Young knew fables spoken by the old!
Within only cruelty, despair was there:
…And so, children stayed away, wildlife had no care!

One child for respect exclaimed, "I am going in":
Others around replied, "goodbye Finn"!
Intrepid entered wood frown upon face:
He wouldn't have if known secret of place!

The rumours were actually based upon fact:
Avoid… because you will disappear, that is that!
hundreds in distant past had ventured into, but none ever return:
Over time, no-entry did all learn!

No reason for woods nature had ever been realised:
Fin: now missing, meant things had to be materialised!
Woods had to be searched, answers to questions provided:
All that would now patrol had to be united, not divided!

After an hour, there came the first cry:
Maybe evidence had be located, as to the disappearance why?
More clues were gathered, but Finn himself not found:
Heads lowered, this as rumours started going around!

Collated was all evidence, but still it told no true facts:
Riddle was not solved, simply lead to many tracks!
Efforts now exhausted, but still no actual Finn:
Endeavour for the cause, this time did not win!

Mysteries are part, parcels that sometimes remain closed:
This of life, where billion a question is posed!
Answers to are the nectar, but bring grievance too:
Peace of mind given to so few!

# TRUE FEAR

After build-up that moment so intense:
When from fear, there is no fence!
Eyes for a moment closed through apprehension:
Darkness of place added to the tension!

That chill that sends body into quiver:
At point when voice, only scream deliver!
Accident down below, this for the few:
Horror upon face: "what if anybody knew"?

Millions brave to watch, thousands at thought of tremble:
Yet even before launch, hundreds assemble!
instigators show up, this to ignite the flame of their desire:
Anticipation of viewing, this their newest life's highwire!

Fear is more common in the sphere of the cinematic:
But what the result when truly climatic?
Real happenings that before your eyes do unfold:
'flight, or fight': paralysed your body on frozen hold!

witness to atrocity, you can only glare:
Not process your brain reactions, just stare!
Seconds are hours, even when aided you are hypnotised:
Speech only blabber, no sentence of comprehension realised!

Time now the governor, head of brain... life to reconnect:
Events of moments then, in time recollect!
Move on, or into anxiety fall:
Move through door or keep hitting the emotional wall!

True fear can come at any point, moment in time:
Is a period of emotional rhyme!
Cinematic, or actual... catalyst of scare all:
Chosen as genre, but reality of... too many under spell of fall!

# TIME OF US

Work on the passion, work on your smile:
If you get it right, we can reconcile!
My heart leapt, this when I saw you for the first time:
Thought you were love's true rhyme!

Two souls touched, as if one:
Ours were the sweetest notes of love's song!
An eternity, but that only two weeks ago:
Perfection was our union, you must know!

Put water did you upon the love flames:
I had the passion, but you had different aims!
We fell deeply in that called love:
Thought our being, heaven sent from above!
At present I sit alone, longing again for your hand:
Burning inside with hope, please understand!
Is this that itch, hesitation before to longevity commit?
Or is it our end, true love you forfeit!

We kissed the first night, we connected then:
Knew from moment, just time for the true physical when!
Palpitations erupted to my very core:
Known in a second, wanted was much more!

But that was then, this is now:
Hesitate do not... this to return us to the wow!
...If only; we could start again:
My very essence at present, feels only pain!

# PROFITABILITY

Profitability… millions from ideas, always can be made:
This always after any monkeys have been paid!
Real money from none, chance of gaining, there is a hope grain:
In truth, most businesses do not get passed the 'three-year pain'!

Established… economic conditions, do decide growth:
How hardships, show business wroth!
That one inspiration, that became a real thing:
Even if smaller, can be loved the most… initiator sing!

Even when no hope, the dream still is not over, and done:
Perhaps more capital investment; could resurrect the start-up fun!
…But who to invest, the banks say no:
Family now, the only route to go!

Who amongst kinfolk have the resources, who would have resolve?
…If fail, what consequences might unfold?
Risk is risk, it must be taken for the money gain idea:
Failure so often, this brings a tear!

Crying is not just if dream ended, though never the aim:
Profitability is not just financial, but also of emotional gain!
Words of inspiration spoken, for brain... itches scratched:
Respect from others, an achievement that cannot be matched:

One foot forward, never a step back:
This is profitability, this is white... never black!
Reach have choices, each their own path:
Hoped is that at end of day, all had a laugh!

# RESPECT OF LIFE

The beach was open, the water so tempting, and clear:
Yet no entry for me, had not been for ten year!
Instead, always watched... allowed others to enjoy the fun:
Did not fear the vast seascape, but in life 'done is done'!

Sometimes even in pleasurable activities, one cannot partake:
Energy levels for fitness, never generate!
The world can offer great success, alternately much bitterness:
At moments we caress, others find hard to process!

The youth have energy, through time so much is lost:
...But life happens, there is always cost!
Injury, illness... perhaps combination of both:
These curtailers of freedom, that all should toast!

It is the energy of the carers... their value
should be respected by all:
In the equation that is humanity, they stand so tall!
Family member, or profession... reverence to you:
Life is enhanced, this by the giving to another by the few!

# TOAST

Toast: even whilst cooking the hunger fangs burn:
Any time of day, most British at least do yearn!
A piece or two of perfection, simply bliss:
Even the poor can afford, pleasure this!

Through aromas others are awoken, soon do they indulge:
From tendrils of sleep soon to evolve!
Back to awareness the world again to embrace:
Food of hand eaten in indulgence, or hast!

Beans, and sausage compliment, so do hundreds of other things:
Known is that eyes widen, mouth sings!
Loved even by children, toast is an easiest quick choice:
Aids the singing, of at least the British voice!

Nutritional deficient, but still a staple course of food:
Buttered is perfection, without would be crude!
Dry toast is eaten, but by those who watch their calorie's:
All I know, is that it always does please!

# COPING MECHANISMS

For each they're different, though have a name:
...But at least in the short-term, ease the pain!
Alcoholism, or self-harming, to name just two:
Both 'coping mechanisms' which allow, life to get through!

When lows occur, started are sparks of... to the light:
Once flaming, they are an individual's right!
Concerned loved ones, against make us want to fight:
...But as to the reason, they have no foresight!

Praying might be answer, for person, or to common cause:
...If sporting event, may bring about great applause!
Upon personal level, religion is still the most populous thing:
It's comfort makes so many hearts sing!

Harmful to body or not, 'coping mechanisms' are reality's theme:
...If success of, or from reason, are life's dream!
Problems put behind, now life again to enjoy, and scheme:
A smile upon face always, and forever gleam!

# AUTUMN NOW

As green's turn to brown's, the temperature falls:
Autumn has arrived, heating needed between your walls!
Outside heavier coverings adorned, to with weather cope:
Bedraggled or not, nature is a game of hope!

Dark races with light, after summer equinox always win:
Artificial luminance vital to light the within!
Severn minutes a day is lost to the dark:
Shortening day rays, allow increasing heard any dog bark!

Bustle of summer… this slows as footfall dwindles:
Time itself, natural heat swindles!
Dead leaf's everywhere, slippery if trod upon:
Wind-blown into clusters, no matter where from!

Though colder, this time for the multitude is a friend:
Ever decreasing incessant insects, their landing at an end!
Now I sit, irritation free:
Cost of life increases, but that's enough for me!

# CANDOUR

Talking in truth, honest and sincere, this is candour:
Evidence honest, to the law trial pander!
With conviction of duty, tell the whole truth:
Jury of twelve, provide with the real proof!

Their candour is to review the evidence given:
Examine in detail, without pre-conviction all written!
Ask for clarification... if anything seems blurred:
Even consider, evidence that might seem absurd!

The barristers candour can be suspect:
Their client winning case, this what they respect!
Monetary concerns, allows stories to be told:
Millions of guilty walk free, this a story of justice so old!

The judges candour, is to rule within confines of the law:
Jury might absolve, but quilt upheld... this if decision poor!
Mistakes happen, each and every day:
Only true candour can put the right ones away!

# THE LONG GAME

Tactically the wrong decision:
loss of pawn is for the long game!
Thinking four moves forward:
Time is the real reality of the aim!

Sacrifice for the greater good:
This concept known by all!
In order to achieve dream of consequence:
billions besides roadside must fall!

Pebbles millions lie in the road:
Any upon loads stutter, over crawl!
Those with real determination make it:
Those without always fall!

Life is simply a crossroads of decision:
Each made ignites our personal path!
A thousand dreams shattered:
Success stories have last laugh!

# FAMILY

This day again I gathered with family:
Sister, brother, and me!
We sat, rejoiced the day:
Now home, but my memories stay!

My sister is brilliant, partner the same:
My family has its game!
Yes, we rejoice in alcohol:
With hundred a story told!

This day was perfect, weather, and rhyme:
Laughed through that clock chime!
'Taking the micky' can be the best thing:
Such in family makes all hearts sing!

Such nonsense that makes laughs appear:
Stupidity that generates thousands of tears!
Family is about being part:
Love, and respect the integral part!

# ABOVE AND BEYOND

Their duties were clear, they abided by the rules:
Had the equipment, all the needed tools!
…But this job, was beyond any other before:
Would be remembered for evermore!

… If completed, would merit much more than applause:
Paraded should be future, this as crowd roars!
Daily challenges are one thing, others come 'out of the blue':
Ten's watch on, but the valiant doo!

Reverence to those that Make the difference:
Only positivity the influence!
Those that aid strangers, throwing 'caution to the wind' be kind:
Humanity at its best, but very few of that bracket find!

Military, or civilian, medals are held in reserve:
Put before own life, they that deserve!
Innocents in real peril, rescued by the truly brave:
So many that would otherwise meet grave!

# BEATING HEARTS FIRE

Give it up for me baby
Your tantalising is driving me crazy
Just a little piece, of what I need right now
Let my being simply be wow

Thunderous rain, echo's my beating heart
you always knew my weakness for you, from the start
the first time I glimpsed you... my body trembled in fear
my future wife, I knew was here

Give it up for me baby
Your tantalising is driving me crazy
Just a little piece, of what I need right now
Let my being simply be wow

Jelly is my body... this when you are close
First time I touched you, I actually froze
Don't know what it is, you enlighten darkened skies
Feat touch earth, but in reality, I do fly

Give it up for me baby
Your tantalising is driving me crazy
Just a little piece of what I need right now
Let my being simply be wow

Our nights, always so gentle… so slow
caresses beneath, and above the throws
giggles, stimulated the very air
naked, passion took us to the ultimate there

Give it up for me baby
Your tantalising is driving me crazy
Just a little piece of what I need right now
Let my being simply be wow

Fallen so deep, no other place to go
Your heat, or isolation of pole
I'll follow anywhere… jump after, if over cliff fell
Even submit to the burning fires of hell

# Acknowledgements

For the poem… Chess:
FIDE: The world ranking organisation.
For the poem… Anniversaries:
Wedding anniversaries year-by-year.
News channels all that have aided my writing.

I also want to thank those that have read this book. Without the reader no literature would mean anything at all. The written paper format may be the oldest, but today writing appears mainly online. Few want the pleasure that is a books aroma. May libraries also be part of humanities venture forward into the unknown!

# Authors final message

If you have read through my poetry, I hope you have a smile upon your face. I write now, but it is hoped that new works by the multitude will never end. Our world is vast, each should be able to have their own say. If upon paper, words will always have something to say!

Printed and bound by CPI Group (UK) Ltd, Croydon, CR0 4YY